INCORPORATION AND BUSINESS GUIDE FOR ALBERTA

INCORPORATION AND BUSINESS GUIDE FOR ALBERTA
How to form your own corporation

David M. Goldenberg, LL.B.

Self-Counsel Press
(*a division of*)
International Self-Counsel Press Ltd.
Canada U.S.A.

Printed in Canada

First edition: January 1972
Tenth edition: February 1993
Eleventh edition: January 1995
Twelfth edition: May 1997

Canadian Cataloguing in Publication Data
Goldenberg, David M.
    Incorporation and business guide for Alberta

    (Self-counsel legal series)
    ISBN 1-55180-132-9

    1. Incorporation — Alberta — Popular works. 2. Private companies — Alberta — Popular works.   I. Title. II. Series.
KEA316.Z82G64 1997   346.7123'06622   C97-910218-9
KF1420.Z9G64 1997

Self-Counsel Press
(*a division of*)
International Self-Counsel Press Ltd.
Head and Editorial Office
1481 Charlotte Road
North Vancouver, BC V7J 1H1

U.S. Address
1704 N. State Street
Bellingham, WA 98255

AVAILABLE FROM THE PUBLISHER

In order to incorporate yourself, you will need to file certain forms. You may type these yourself, but it is easier and quicker to use pre-printed forms or software, if you wish, you can take advantage of our typing service and have all the forms completed for you.

PLAN No. 1

Incorporation forms only — $12.95

Some of these forms are available from the Companies Branch, but the long, typed forms, such as the by-laws, are not and many people like the convenience of using pre-printed forms, which saves considerably on the time and expense of typing. The forms are available where you bought this book or you may use the order form on page vii. The cost of each package is $12.95.

The set includes:

Articles of Incorporation
By-laws
Share certificates
Notice of Directors
Notice of Address
Resolution of Directors
Resolution of Shareholders

PLAN No. 2

Typing Service — $100.00

We offer a typing service that is as easy as picking up the phone and calling our toll-free number, 1-800-663-3007. Please read this book carefully before you call.

If you have decided to incorporate a small, non-distributing corporation, here's how we can help:

1. We will take your name and address and mail Incorporation Data sheets out to you for you to complete.

2. You reserve the name with the Companies Branch (see page 26). (We have found this to be faster than if we do it.)

3. You return the completed data sheets to us. We will then type all the documents and return them to you for filing with the Companies Branch.

4. We cannot give you legal advice but will assist you in the filing process where possible.

After reading this book, you are in an informed position and are at liberty to choose whether or not you want to make use of this service. The publication is complete in itself and you can handle your own incorporation without using this extra service. However, many people prefer a little assistance or are willing to pay for the convenience.

Your documents will be completed by competent personnel, but we cannot and we do not give legal advice. If you have complicated tax or incorporation problems, we recommend that you see an experienced lawyer.

PLAN No. 3

Software — $35.00

Our *Incorporation Self-Ware* enables you to incorporate a company right on your own PC (see order form on the next page).

Features

- Stand-alone software, no word-processing package is required
- Easy to install
- Menu driven
- Built-in error checking helps ensure
- Pop-up help screens provide definitions of legal terms and explanations of important concepts
- Mouse or keyboard driven
- Free technical support available to all registered owners

System Requirements

- IBM/Tandy/100% compatible computer
- 512K RAM free
- Floppy and hard disk drives
- DOS 3.3 or higher papers are complete
- Supports any standard printer

This software is intended for use on a single computer, by a single user only.

ADDITIONAL ITEMS AVAILABLE FROM THE PUBLISHER

Company seal, up to 39 characters — $35.00

Company seal, 40 or more characters — $40.00

(The seal should not be ordered until you have received your Certificate of Incorporation.)

Minute book — $17.95

Deposit stamp — "For Deposit Only to the Credit of _____" — $14.25

Endorsement stamp — "Company Name" — $10.50

Name and address stamp — $16.95

Note: Please allow 3 to 4 weeks for delivery.

Prices are subject to change without notice.

Send to:
Self-Counsel Press
1481 Charlotte Road
North Vancouver, BC V7J 1H1

(Clip and mail)

- - - - - - - - - - - - - - - **ORDER FORM** - - - - - - - - - - - - - - -

Please send the following items prepaid:

_____	Package form kit	$12.95
_____	Seal, up to 39 characters	$35.00
_____	Seal, 40 or more characters	$40.00
_____	Minute book	$17.95
_____	Incorporation software	$35.00
_____	Deposit stamp	$14.25
_____	Endorsement stamp	$10.50
_____	Name and address stamp	$16.95
_____	Extra share certificates — 50¢ each	_____

Add $2.80 for postage and handling books, kits, etc.   _____

Add $3.00 postage and handling for seals and stamps, if ordered   _____

Subtotal   _____

Add 7% GST calculated on subtotal   _____

TOTAL amount to be forwarded by money order   _____

Or, if you prefer, you can charge it to your MasterCard or Visa. Please fill in number, expiry date, and validation date (if MasterCard) below.

All prices subject to change without notice.

Please send the items checked above to: *(Please print)*

Mr./Ms. _____

Address: _____

City: _____ Province: _____

Postal code:_____ Telephone: _____

Name of corporation: _____

Corporation address (for stamp) if not same as above:_____

_____

MasterCard/Visa number:_____Expiry date: _____

Validation date: _____ Signature: _____

Please check your seals and stamps upon receipt. We will not be responsible for errors reported more than 30 days after mailing.

Incorporation Software: To ensure you have all the relevant information to incorporate your company, you must use this form to place your order. We are unable to fill software orders unless this form is used.

INCALTA 12/97

NOTICE TO READERS

CONTENTS

SAMPLES

PREFACE

The purpose of this book is to provide enough legal and practical information about incorporating a company so you can incorporate a company under the Alberta Business Corporations Act.

The book explains in layperson's language the basic procedures necessary for incorporating and setting up your company. It is recommended that if procedures of a more sophisticated nature are required, you seek competent legal and accounting advice.

By following the steps in this book, you will save a substantial amount ($500 to $600) in lawyer's fees for incorporating a company.

Whether or not you seek competent professional help prior to incorporation, you will undoubtedly require the services of a qualified accountant and/or lawyer following incorporation.

This publication is not meant to downgrade the value of professional help. It is meant as an aid to people who want to incorporate and find that the money spent for professional fees may be better spent elsewhere, or for those who simply want to become acquainted with the legal and practical implications of a limited company.

INTRODUCTION

Congratulations!

Congratulations for what, you may ask. Congratulations for entering into the exciting world of business.

If you read this book, you obviously do so with the intention of obtaining some tips on how to organize and manage a business venture. You have probably already made the major decision to go into business, which will usually involve giving up the security of a job, a guaranteed income, and an existing way of life. There will be few decisions of more importance that you will make in your life.

The purpose of this book is to help you chart your course toward many successful years in Alberta's business community from the earliest decisions about the type of business to operate, through the set-up procedure, and into actually running the business. It is designed to assist you in properly structuring your business in order to maximize profits and minimize cost.

This book has been written in lay language and is designed to provide you with brief explanations of why things have to be done as well as how to do them.

The overall emphasis is on companies and the incorporation procedure. The words "company" and "corporation" are interchangeable. But no matter how they are described, companies, as you will see, are an interesting and flexible tool available to you. A thorough understanding of how they operate will be of great benefit throughout the life of your business.

a. THE ACT

When it came into effect, the Alberta Business Corporations Act simplified the procedure for incorporating and allowed one-person companies, which increased the appeal of incorporating to many people. The Business Corporations Act went into effect on February 1, 1982. If you would like to have a copy of the act, which is always helpful for reference, you may order it from:

Print Graphic Services
601, 620 — 7th Avenue S.W.
Calgary, AB T2P 0Y8

As you might imagine, quite an involved bureaucracy has been created to administer the Business Corporations Act and oversee the companies operating under it.

The head office for this department is a branch of the Department of Consumer and Corporate Affairs, the Corporate Registry, which is sometimes called the Companies Branch. It is located in Edmonton at the following addresses:

Corporate Registry
Alberta Consumer and Corporate Affairs
8th Floor, John E. Brownlee Bldg.
10365 — 97 Street
Edmonton, AB T5J 3W7
Telephone: (403) 427-2311
Fax: (403) 422 1091
OR:
Box 1007
Main Post Office
Edmonton, AB T5J 4W6

The head office maintains public hours and will take telephone inquiries up to 3 p.m. A 24-hour touch-tone telephone service is also available.

Any member of the public can obtain information about an existing company in a search request asking the date of incorporation, the names of directors and shareholders, the location of the registered office, and whether the corporation is in good standing. There is a standard charge of $10 per search. Expedited service is available upon request at no extra charge.

The Companies Branch maintains records on microfiche, and searches can be made personally at the Edmonton office for a fee of $10 per company. You will then be entitled to examine all the documents filed with the Companies Branch, which include the Articles of Incorporation and continuance documents, and any amendments to those documents.

The person in charge of the Companies Branch is the Registrar of Companies. The Registrar has some discretionary powers under the act, including the discretion to refuse a name or to require an existing company to change its name.

The Registrar also has the power to dissolve a corporation or attach conditions to the revival of a corporation.

Working under the Registrar's supervision are a number of assistants, supervisors, document examiners, and a large support staff. They have limited discretion in certain areas they are working in, such as name approvals, continuance documentation, incorporations, and renewals.

Although this area of law and administration is growing very rapidly, the Registrar and assistants are still accessible to the public by telephone or by letter. Therefore, if you have a question, complaint, or even a bouquet, you can contact the Registrar or one of the many assistants or supervisors.

The general aim of the Business Corporations Act is to allow a corporation the flexibility and authority it needs to run its own affairs without intervention by administrative officials or by the courts. However, the Business Corporations Act has also been designed to provide safeguards for shareholders and creditors. To that extent at least, the law gives wide power to the courts, which in certain instances could lead to changes in the Articles of Incorporation or even a unanimous shareholder agreement. If you are ever involved in a situation that involves, or could involve, court action, legal advice is recommended.

b. THE ORGANIZATION OF THIS BOOK

The table of contents in this book is designed to be a quick reference and an outline of the topics discussed inside. You'll find references to specific items that may be of interest to you.

This book is divided into ten chapters. This first chapter is a painless introduction to the topic, including both a brief overview of the administration of the system and some information on the current law in Alberta.

Interspersed throughout the book are examples illustrating various points of interest. Because corporations must file certain documents with the government and keep good records, samples of all the relevant forms are included where required.

Chapters 2 to 6 provide the meat of the book; they go through the entire life of a corporation from birth until death or dissolution. Just as an individual grows, learns, and changes, so does a company; just as a child's parents normally constitute the greatest influence on an offspring through its formative years, you will see that the creators of a company — its shareholders — exert a similar influence.

In chapter 7 you'll learn how your company may carry on business in other provinces or transfer its base from provincial to federal or vice versa.

Chapters 8 and 9 discuss some "non-legal" but very important considerations involved in business. Topics include tax matters, municipal, provincial, and federal licensing requirements, and financing opportunities.

Chapter 10 contains a few concluding remarks about the general nature of this most unusual, but extremely important creation, the corporation.

Note: By early 1986, all companies that were incorporated prior to February, 1982 have either been "continued" under the Alberta Business Corporations Act or have been automatically dissolved for failure to continue. The continuance process was designed to allow companies incorporated prior to the introduction of the Alberta Business Corporations Act to refile with Corporate Registry to retain their legal right to carry on business in Alberta. Legislation provided that if a corporation did not continue within the requisite time period, it would automatically be dissolved.

The provision did allow for a dissolved corporation to "revive" itself through an application to court. If you have a company that was not properly continued and has, therefore, been dissolved, you should obtain legal advice about properly reviving your corporation.

1

WHAT YOU SHOULD KNOW ABOUT BUSINESS, CORPORATIONS, AND CORPORATE LAW

a. METHODS OF CARRYING ON BUSINESS

1. Introduction

From earliest times until today, there have basically been three ways in which a person or persons could carry on business. As society has become more complex, manners and modes of carrying on business have also changed, but the three basic forms survive and are, in essence, the foundation of all business activity. Those ways of carrying on business are known as the sole proprietorship, the partnership, and incorporation.

2. Sole proprietorships

Any individual who carries on a business activity alone and without the use of a limited company carries on business, by definition, as a sole proprietor. This does not mean that you need use your own name in the business. In fact, the majority of sole proprietors carry on business using another name, which they hope will attract customers or business in one way or another.

Accordingly, Joe Smith who operates an auto repair shop may use the name "Joe's Quick Repairs" and still be operating as a sole proprietor. This is a perfectly legal way of doing business unless the use of the name "Joe's Quick Repairs" is in some way designed to confuse the public and "pass off" onto Mr. Smith any of the benefits that another business has built up over a period of time because of a similar name. For example, Mr. Smith would get into trouble if he attempted to use the name "General Motor Repairs" because of the obvious attempt to cash in on the association with "General Motors."

If legal action has to be taken by or against a sole proprietor, the sole proprietor may be personally named in the lawsuit or may be sued under the trade name.

Legally, the sole proprietor owns all of the assets of the business and is personally responsible for all its liabilities. All the income generated by the business is treated as income of the sole proprietor and will ultimately be taxed together with his or her other sources of income at that individual's personal tax rate. When the proprietor dies or retires, the business dies or retires with him or her.

A sole proprietorship is the simplest of all businesses to set up. It requires no legal filings except for a Declaration of Trade Name, which will protect the use of the name from others who may wish to use it in the future. See Sample #1 for a copy of the Declaration as to Trade Name for "Joe's Quick Repairs."

This form is filed for a fee of $30 at the Corporate Registry. Of all of the ways of carrying on business, this method involves the least amount of government interference and may be perfectly functional for you in the early stages of business.

3. Partnerships

A partnership involves a business relationship between two or more parties who carry on business for the purpose of making a profit.

1

SAMPLE #1
DECLARATION OF TRADE NAME

I, ___Joe Smith___ of the ___City of Calgary___ in the Province of Alberta, HEREBY CERTIFY:

1. That we are carrying on or intend to carry on trade and business as ___Joe's Quick Repairs___ in the ___City of Calgary___ in the Province of Alberta, under the name of:

    Joe's Quick Repairs

2. That no other person or persons are associated with me in the said business.

3. That the said business has been carried on under the said name of ___Joe's Quick Repairs___ since the _1st_ day of ___March___, 199- .

DATED at the ___City of Calgary___ in the Province of Alberta, this_10th_ day of ___April___, 199- .

Joe's Quick Repairs
(Name of Corporation)

Per: Joe Smith

Joe Smith

FOR TRADE NAME REGISTRATION WITHIN THE PROVINCE OF ALBERTA

The "profit" aspect is important because two or more individuals can also form associations, societies, or clubs, the prime purpose of which is not to generate a profit but to promote recreational, social, or cultural activities. These are not legally recognized as profit-oriented partnerships.

Partnerships are a creature of legal contract but, surprising as it may seem, these contracts can be implied as well as expressed and oral as well as written. Therefore, many partnerships exist despite the fact that the partners have not entered into a formal written partnership agreement.

Subject to any rules governing particular professions, partnerships may use names other than the names of the partners, and the comments regarding trade names of sole proprietors apply to partnerships as well. Partnerships should also file a Declaration of Trade Name at the Corporate Registry (see Sample #1).

All questions about the structure, formation, creation, and dissolution of partnerships are governed by the Partnership Act of the Province of Alberta. This is a provincial statute based largely on similar legislation across Canada and in Britain. Because of the length of time this legislation has been in existence there are a large number of legal precedents that are in force and which govern the operation of partnerships. While there are no established or definitive tests, the act does set out specific guidelines that can help you answer many questions you may have about partnerships.

A particularly important characteristic of partnerships is that all of the assets owned by the partnership are in fact owned jointly and severally by each of its individual partners. Conversely, all liabilities of the partnership are the liabilities of each partner, and each member of the partnership is designated as the lawful agent of its other partners.

For example, if three individuals are carrying on business as an engineering partnership, all three of the individuals are fully liable for the debts owed by the partnership to the partnership creditors, such as the bank or the landlord.

In addition, because of the partnership designation, if any one of the partners enters into a contract with an outside third party on behalf of the partnership (say for $10 000 worth of engineering equipment), all of the partners become jointly and individually responsible for the repayment of that debt. If partners do not wish this type of risk, it must be expressed in a written partnership agreement and made clear to the third-party creditor.

From a tax point of view, the assets and liabilities of a partnership flow down to the individual partners and, in general, there is no taxation of the partnership entity itself. Specific tax information about partnerships is beyond the scope of this book.

In this day and age of tax shelters, a variation of the partnership concept has become very popular. It is known as the "limited partnership." A limited partnership is a business organization involving one or more general partners and one or more limited partners. The general partner (which is usually a limited company) is responsible for the management and operation of the partnership business. It has unlimited liability for all the partnership debts just as if it were a partner in an ordinary partnership. Limited partners, however, are normally limited in liability to the amount of their initial partnership contribution. In return for this special protection, they are not entitled to take any active role in the management or operation of the partnership business. They are required to be passive investors only.

Because of certain tax incentives created to encourage exploration and development in the oil and gas industry and to encourage new investment in the construction industry, certain flow-through and other tax savings write-offs have been made available to limited partners who invest in limited partnerships. A more detailed examination of them is beyond the scope of this book. You should examine each proposal in detail prior to becoming involved in it, both from a tax point of view and, more importantly, from an investment point of view.

Although the Partnership Act does not require the formal filing of any documents for a general partnership, the act does require the filing of a partnership declaration with the Corporate Registry if the partnership intends to carry on a business in the manufacturing, retail, or trading fields. See Sample #2, which illustrates a typical Declaration of Partnership agreement for the engineering firm mentioned earlier.

Any amendments to the Declaration of Partnership must be recorded in the Amendment to Declaration of Partnership (see Sample #3). The form is available from the Corporate Registry.

The significance of this registration is that from the date of registration, the partnership has priority to use the partnership name over any other sole proprietors or partnerships who wish to carry on business under a similar name.

To create a limited partnership, a Certificate of Limited Partnership must be filed with the Corporate Registry in Alberta setting out specific information regarding the partnership. Sample #4 is a typical Certificate of Limited Partnership. These documents can become quite complex depending on the nature of the limited partnership. If you are considering investing in a limited partnership, review all documents carefully and consider asking for professional assistance from a lawyer or accountant.

Many businesses are carried on as a "joint venture," and although it is recognized as a form of business association in all business circles, the term "joint venture" has never been legally recognized. In fact, the best way of defining a joint venture is simply to call it a partnership in which the participants do not wish to be called or considered partners. The basic difference between the two lies in the different tax considerations involved which, especially in the oil and gas industry, can be quite significant.

Joint venture agreements are in almost all cases written contracts with the rights and liabilities of all the parties clearly expressed. Therefore, the normal laws of contract and contractual interpretation apply in determining the legal rights and remedies of the parties involved.

4. Corporations

The third and most popular method of carrying on business is through the use of the "limited liability corporation" normally referred to as a "company" or "corporation."

Unlike sole proprietorships or partnerships, a corporation is a separate and distinct legal entity, which is created (and destroyed) by statute. Accordingly, unless all of the proper legal requirements, form filings, and other nuisances are complied with and maintained, the corporation simply will never be created or can be involuntarily dissolved.

The single most important characteristic of a company is that it is a separate legal entity. The use of the word "limited" at the end of most existing company names is no accident; it means that the owners of the company, its shareholders, are not in the same position as partners or sole proprietors. They are not totally and completely liable for the debts of the company but are protected from its debts. In fact, the maximum amount of the liability for the shareholder in a company is the initial amount that he or she paid for shares. If the company suffers losses and goes under, the shareholder simply loses his or her initial investment and nothing more. As we have seen, this is completely different from the sole proprietor or partner who has unlimited liability to creditors of the business.

The concept of limited liability is fundamental to an understanding of how companies work. Throughout the balance of this chapter and the remaining chapters of this book, you will become more and more familiar with many of the other distinct characteristics of companies. You need only be aware of the tremendous number of companies currently in business in Alberta to know that a company can be a very valuable tool in successfully operating your business.

b. AN INTRODUCTION TO CORPORATIONS

1. Historical development

For several reasons, the development of companies has contributed to the great expansion of commerce in our society. The notion of the separation of ownership and management, which is fundamental to incorporation, has created a special class of experienced managers whose skills are vital in running a business. On the other hand, the system allows individuals with capital but without expertise or the desire to become involved in management to simply act as investors with the goal of getting a healthy return on that investment.

Our system of corporate law derives from British common law. It has developed gradually over the years to the point where we have now developed a distinct Canadian law. Because the business world involves rapid changes, corporate law is also continually changing and growing.

2. Advantages and disadvantages of incorporation

We have already noted that limited liability is one of the major advantages of incorporation. For example, imagine that you are operating a sole proprietorship and incur a $50 000 debt with a supplier. If the business fails, you will be personally liable to that supplier for the $50 000 debt; any assets that you own, which may or may not be part of the business, such as your home, automobile, etc., may be seized by that creditor to satisfy the debt.

If you operate through a company, and it is the company that validly incurs the $50 000 debt, the creditor's action is against the company only. Unless that creditor can prove fraud of one form or another, you will not have any personal liability except to the extent of your initial purchase price of the shares. Your personal assets will be safeguarded from possible seizure by the creditor.

Other advantages to incorporation are as follows:

(a) Like most business people, one of your prime goals is probably to maximize the amount of monies that you take home with you at the end of each working day. In 1917, the federal government introduced a temporary piece of legislation known as "income tax," which has managed somehow to remain on the books. This notion of paying taxes has become ingrained in our daily way of life.

   However, incorporating provides you with certain tax benefits that are not otherwise available; in fact, the tax savings available through incorporation can be the largest single advantage to incorporating, especially in the province of Alberta. (See chapter 8 for specific tax benefits.)

(b) Unlike partnerships and sole proprietorships, a company does not cease to exist upon the death of one of the individuals involved. Because it is a separate legal entity, it continues in existence despite the death of the controlling shareholder. This notion of continuity is especially important in businesses that have long-term obligations and income opportunities.

(c) Another advantage of incorporation that I am particularly impressed with is the potential for unlimited flexibility and the opportunities for creativity that are provided to those who wish to use them. A partnership or even sole proprietorship is often structured and static, while a company can change, grow, or adapt with the changing times.

The main disadvantage associated with incorporation compared to other methods of carrying on business is the requirement of increased administration, accounting, and government supervision. Forms must be filed with the government from time to time, and the initial set-up of a corporation can be time-consuming and, even if you do it yourself, more costly than the set-up of a partnership or sole proprietorship.

As well, the creation of a separate legal entity creates a new client for your accountant or bookkeeper so that additional record keeping expenses are involved. Annual financial statements, along with federal and provincial income tax filings are normally required. However, those disadvantages are normally minor compared to benefits available through incorporation.

3. Who may incorporate?

As you will see in chapters 2 and 3, one person alone can set up and run a corporation. Because a corporation is defined as a person, a company can legally incorporate another company.

The legislation does not state any qualifications for an incorporator, such as age, mental competence, or financial solvency. There are other restrictions, such as residency requirements for directors, which will be discussed in later chapters.

DECLARATION OF PARTNERSHIP

PROVINCE OF ALBERTA

WE, ___Sly D. Ruler___, AND ___D. Raftsman___ of the City of ___Calgary___, in the Province of Alberta, HEREBY CERTIFY:

1. THAT we are carrying on or intend to carry on trade and business as ___engineering consultants___, in partnership under the name of ___Prairie Engineering___.

2. THAT the said Partnership has subsisted since the ___1st___ day of ___April___ A.D., ___199-___.

3. AND THAT we are and have been since the said day the only members of the said partnership.

WITNESS OUR HANDS AT ___Calgary___, Alberta, this ___15th___ day of ___May___ A.D., ___199-___.

Name and address and occupation of partners and each one has to sign.

Sly D. Ruler
1234 A Avenue
Calgary AB T1O 1O1
Engineer

D. Raftsman
4321 B Street
Calgary AB T2Z 2Z2
Engineer

Sly D. Ruler

D. Raftsman

SAMPLE #3
AMENDMENT TO DECLARATION OF PARTNERSHIP

AMENDMENT TO DECLARATION OF PARTNERSHIP
PROVINCE OF ALBERTA

NAME OF PARTNERSHIP:___PRAIRIE ENGINEERING_____

REGISTRATION NUMBER:___555ZZTOP_____

We, the persons named as partners in the Declaration, HEREBY DECLARE:

1. THAT the name of the Partnership has been changed to:

    FREEFALL ENGINEERING_____

    from:
    PRAIRIE ENGINEERING_____

2. THAT the current partners are:
    a. NAME:__Sly D. Ruler_____
        RESIDENT ADDRESS:__1234 A Avenue, Calgary, Alberta____

        SIGNATURE:_____
        _____Sly D. Ruler_____

    b. NAME:__D. Raftsman_____
        RESIDENT ADDRESS:__4321 B Street, Calgary, Alberta____

        SIGNATURE:_____
        _____

3. DO THE NAMES ABOVE REFLECT A CHANGE OF PARTNERS?__NO__
4. DATE OF DECLARATION:__September 15, 19-_____

NOTE: AMENDMENTS TO THE DECLARATION OF PARTNERSHIP MUST BE SIGNED BY ALL MEMBERS OF THE PARTNERSHIP AND MUST STATE ONLY THE CHANGE THAT HAS TAKEN PLACE.

SAMPLE #4
CERTIFICATE OF LIMITED PARTNERSHIP

IN THE MATTER OF THE PARTNERSHIP ACT
BEING CHAPTER   OF THE REVISED STATUTES
OF ALBERTA, 1981 AND AMENDMENTS THERETO

CERTIFICATE OF LIMITED PARTNERSHIP

WE, THE UNDERSIGNED GENERAL PARTNER AND LIMITED PARTNERS DO HEREBY CERTIFY THAT:

1.   The firm name and style under which the Limited Partnership is conducted is "DYNAMIC CONSULTING ENGINEERS."

2.   The Partnership is established for the purposes of:

(a)   Carrying on the business of consulting engineers and related services;

(b)   Acquiring for cash or for an interest in the Partnership or both, or otherwise as the Partners may determine, any property, movable or immovable, rights, leases, businesses, franchises, undertakings, powers, privileges, licenses, patents, patent rights, concessions, shares, stocks, bonds, debentures, debenture stock or choses-in-action which the General Partner may deem are appropriate to be acquired by the Partnership as being incidental to or ancillary to the business of the Partnership and any of its objects;

(c)   Obtaining such financing as the Partners deem may be required to achieve the above objects of the Partnership and to conduct the business of the Partnership;

(d)   Guaranteeing the payment or performance of any debts, contracts, or obligations whatsoever, or to become surety for any person, firm, corporation or company for any purpose whatsoever;

(e)   Borrowing, raising or securing the payment of money in such manner as the Partners may think fit (including but so as not to restrict the generality of the foregoing) by mortgage, charge, hypothecation or pledge of or upon all or any of the Partnership's property, both present and future in order to achieve the above objects and to carry on the business of the Partnership;

(f)   Entering into any and all contracts and arrangements whatsoever for the purpose of achieving any of the above objects of the Partnership, and in the conduct of the business of the Partnership;

(g)   Carrying on any trade or business whatsoever which, in the opinion of the Partners as determined by resolution at a general meeting of the Partners, can be carried on lawfully and advantageously by the Partnership in connection with or ancillary to any of the above.

AND IT IS HEREBY DECLARED that in the interpretation of this paragraph, the scope and meaning of any of the above, no inference as to their relative importance shall be drawn from their respective position in the list of the above, nor shall the meaning of any of the above be restricted by reference to, or inference from, any other items, or the name of the Partnership, or by the juxtaposition of two or more of the above items and in the event of any ambiguity each clause of this paragraph shall be construed in such manner as to widen and not to restrict the objects or business of the Partnership and its powers to achieve those objects and to conduct its business.

3.   The names and places of residence of the General Partner and the Limited Partners are as follows:

A.   GENERAL PARTNER

STEAMPIPE ENGINEERING LTD., a body corporate under the laws of the Province of Alberta, with an office at 124-100 Street, Edmonton, Alberta T6H 2L6

B.   LIMITED PARTNERS

Attached as per Schedule "A" to this Certificate is a list of the names and registered offices of the Limited Partners.

4.   The Limited Partnership is to continue indefinitely until the Limited Partnership is terminated by either the unanimous resolution of the Partners passed at a meeting of the Partners called for that purpose or, secondly, by the agreement in writing of all the Partners to that effect. The withdrawal, for any reason whatsoever, of a Limited Partner shall not terminate the Limited Partnership so long as there remains at least two (2) Partners in the Limited Partnership. The General Partner may not under any circumstances withdraw from the Limited Partnership or cease to be a Partner in the Limited Partnership unless the Limited Partnership is terminated.

5.   The amount of the contribution to be made by each of the Limited Partners is ONE HUNDRED ($100.00) DOLLARS.

6.   The amount of additional contributions, if any, and the times at which such additional contributions are to be made by each of the Limited Partners have not been agreed upon.

7.   The time when the contribution of each Limited Partner is to be returned to that Limited Partner has not been agreed upon, except that it shall be returned within six (6) months after the end of the fiscal year of the Partnership in which that Partner ceased to be a member of the Partnership.

8.   The shares of profits or other compensation by way of income which the Partners are entitled to are as follows:

Profits and losses of the Partnership are shared or borne, as the case may be, in a ratio or according to a formula that is established by resolution of the Partners.

9.   A Limited Partner has no right to substitute an assignee as Partner in his place unless unanimously consented to in writing by the other Partners.

10.   The right of the Partners to admit additional Limited Partners is as follows:

A new Limited Partner may be admitted to the Partnership by a unanimous resolution of the Partnership at a meeting called for that purpose, which resolution shall specify the terms and conditions upon which such new Partners shall be admitted to the Partnership.

11.   There is no right of any of the Limited Partners to priority over other Limited Partners to a return of contributions or to compensation by way of income from the Limited Partnership.

12. There is no right of a Limited Partner to demand and receive property other than cash in return for its contribution to the Limited Partnership.

IN WITNESS WHEREOF the General Partner has hereunto affixed its corporate seal as attested by its proper officer in that behalf, and the Limited Partners have hereunto set their seals as attested to by their proper officers in their respective behalves, this 1st day of April, 199-.

GENERAL PARTNER: STEAMPIPE ENGINEERING LTD.

Per: *Phyllis Phulton*

Per: *Steven Steam*

Per: *Peter Piper*

LIMITED PARTNERS: HEALTHY & WEALTHY ENGINEERING LTD.

Per: *Wally Wise*

CROOKED LINE ENGINEERING LTD.

Per: *G. Strait*

SPACE AGE ENGINEERING &
CONSULTANTS LTD.

Per: *S. S. Kye*

SCHEDULE "A"

NAMES AND REGISTERED OFFICES OF LIMITED PARTNERS

Healthy & Wealthy Engineering Ltd.	#100-1234 Jasper Avenue Edmonton, Alberta
Crooked Line Engineering Ltd.	6789-40 Street Edmonton, Alberta
Space Age Engineering & Consultants Ltd.	#10B-1015-109 Street Edmonton, Alberta

2
PRE-INCORPORATION CONSIDERATIONS

a. INTRODUCTION

After you have made your decision to incorporate, there are a number of questions that will come to mind; until those questions are properly answered, the actual incorporation should not be done. This chapter will identify and answer those questions and, in doing so, will provide you with a brief but necessary introduction to some of the concepts and ideas that are part of corporate law. Once these questions have been answered to your satisfaction and you are familiar with those concepts, doing the incorporation procedure is easy.

b. WHERE DO I INCORPORATE?

We begin with the initial assumption that you wish to have your company carry on business in the province of Alberta. This can be accomplished through either a federally incorporated company or a provincially incorporated company. What are the differences?

One of the reasons for the new Business Corporations Act was to create uniformity in dealing with the administration of corporations throughout Canada. In actual fact, there are not a lot of differences, from a legal point of view, between incorporating federally or provincially.

The main differences centre on the questions of cost, jurisdiction, and corporate name. A federally incorporated company is by law entitled to carry on business in every province of Canada, while an Alberta incorporated company is entitled only to carry on business in Alberta. This advantage, however, is not as significant as

it may sound. For a federal company to be legally empowered to carry on business in a province, it must register in that province just as if it had been incorporated in another province (see chapter 7 on extra-provincial registration). Therefore, even a federally incorporated company that wants to do business outside the province of Alberta or borrow funds outside the province of Alberta would probably be required to register in that other province.

Federal companies do maintain a priority with regard to corporate names to the extent that a name may be refused to a company wishing to incorporate provincially if the name or one very similar to it is already in use by a federal corporation. For example, say Priscilla Pinn wished to incorporate in Alberta under the name of Pinn Acupuncture Clinic Ltd. and there was already a federally incorporated company known as Pinn Acupuncture Centre Ltd. Even if the federal company operated only in Newfoundland, the Alberta name would be in jeopardy of either not being approved or, at the very least, subject to being forced to change its name if the federal corporation complained that the names were confusing in the mind of the public.

Similarly, if a name is approved federally and the company registers in another province besides the one in which its head office is located, it will effectively corner the market on the use of that name in the second province.

The major disadvantage of incorporating federally is the distance you may be from the bureaucrats who are administering

12

your company. With a provincially incorporated company, most of the information that you need can be readily obtained in either Calgary or Edmonton, and all searches, reservations of names, etc., can be done relatively quickly. However, to be fair, the federal system seems to be operating quite efficiently and this does not pose the serious problem that was anticipated when the new federal system went into effect.

Further, it costs more to incorporate federally. Currently, registration costs for a federal corporation are $500, but only $300 for an Alberta corporation. With federal incorporation, you will have to pay extra-provincial registration costs for your company to carry on business in Alberta.

The type of company that you will be setting up will probably lend itself more to a provincial registration than federal in that it is unlikely that you will be spreading your business to more than one or two jurisdictions outside Alberta. As well, the chances of obtaining the name you want will be easier going through the Alberta Companies Branch. Accordingly, unless there is some compelling reason to go for federal incorporation, my suggestion would be to incorporate provincially.

c. WHO ARE THE PEOPLE BEHIND COMPANIES?

1. The "many hats" theory

Many people do not realize that the basic structure of the smallest one-person company is basically identical to the structure of the largest public corporation in existence.

The major difference, besides the obvious one of income and profit, is that in the larger corporations, different people are involved in different aspects of the company. Therefore, IBM has its own board of directors, its own extensive management team and executives as well as hundreds of thousands of shareholders throughout the world who have invested in the company. Your company will have exactly the same characteristics except that, in all likelihood, you will be handling all of those various roles, i.e., shareholder, director, officer, and probably employee and creditor of the company.

I refer to this phenomenon as the "many hats" theory because you as the prime mover and organizer of the corporation will wear many hats in carrying on your business. In order to understand how the business is or should be run, it is necessary to examine the various hats that are worn and the duties, liabilities, and obligations attached to each.

2. Shareholders — rights, duties, and liabilities

Shareholders are those individuals (or corporations) who provide the capital necessary to allow the business to commence and continue operation. Shareholders contribute their investment capital to the company by purchasing shares. Those funds are then used by the directors and officers of the company to run the business.

It is important to note that shareholders, wearing their "shareholders' hats," have no say in the control or management of the company but are, in fact, passive investors. If the managers of the company do not perform their duties properly, the shareholders have the right from time to time to replace them. This would normally occur at the annual general meeting. As well, under the Business Corporations Act, shareholders have the right to be bought out of the company if the directors of the company propose a fundamental change. Chapter 6 will discuss this concept of fundamental change in more detail.

Shareholders, unlike directors, owe no duty to the company. While wearing the hat of a shareholder, your biggest concern is for yourself: you hope that you make money, either from the increase in your share value or from dividends. As well, the shareholder, while wearing this hat, is not liable for any of the debts of the company (remember the concept of limited liability discussed in chapter 1).

The company is obliged to hold at least one "annual shareholders' meeting" each year and may hold special shareholders' meetings from time to time. (See chapter 6). At the annual shareholders' meeting, the shareholders are to be provided with certain financial information of the company as well as an update on the company's activities for the past and forthcoming year. It is at this annual meeting that the shareholders have the power to elect the board of directors for the forthcoming year. Once the directors have been elected, however, the management and the control of the business rest with them.

3. Directors — rights, duties, and liabilities

In large public corporations, the board of directors usually consists of two groups. The first is a group of professional managers who have certain expertise in the particular business involved and can be of assistance in planning the operations of the company. The second is usually a group of well-known individuals who can lend some prestige to the company.

Both of those groups comprise the board of directors and are elected by the shareholders at the annual shareholders' meeting. They are charged with the responsibility of managing the business and, depending on the size of the company, may do everything from the actual day-to-day business operations to simply charting the direction of the company and delegating the actual work to other individuals.

The board of directors in your company has exactly the same functions. If you analyze the situation, the criteria upon which you will elect your members to the board will be based on the same considerations that are made by large public companies, although I would suspect that the attribute of expertise, at this stage of the business at any rate, may be more important than the prestige a new person could bring to the board.

You also probably feel that you are the one who knows most about the business that you are putting together. As well, you probably have more faith in yourself than anybody else to handle the job. Accordingly, in most situations, you as the prime shareholder will elect yourself to the board of directors.

Once on the board, however, you will be wearing a different hat, one that has some very significant legal responsibilities and duties, especially under the terms of the Business Corporations Act.

Anybody can be elected as a director as long as he or she is over 18 years of age, not of unsound mind, and not officially in bankruptcy (although there is no reason why a person discharged from bankruptcy cannot act a director). A body corporate may not act as a director, and unless the articles of a company otherwise provide, a director is not required to hold shares issued by the company.

It is also very important to note that at least one-half of the directors of a corporation must be resident Canadians. Resident Canadians are defined as individuals who are ordinarily resident in Canada or have been lawfully admitted to Canada for permanent residency. Without this requirement being fulfilled, directors may not transact business except to appoint a replacement director following the death or resignation of a director.

In chapter 4, we will discuss in detail the actual mechanics involved in the election of directors, the directors' meetings, and quorums. This chapter is designed simply to introduce you to the rights, duties, and obligations that a director has.

Under the Business Corporations Act, the directors of a corporation have the inherent power, without shareholder approval, to borrow money on the credit of the corporation, give a guarantee on behalf of the corporation to secure debts, or to mortgage, pledge, or otherwise create a security on any of the property of the company in order to secure a corporate debt. Chapter 9 covers what is involved in "securing a debt."

Directors also have the right to delegate certain powers to a committee of directors or to a managing director, who must be a resident Canadian.

Unlike shareholders, however, directors do have specific duties toward the company. In law, they are considered to be in a position of trust (fiduciary duty) in favor of the company, and the Business Corporations Act has increased the duty of care that directors (and officers) have.

Every director must act honestly and in good faith with a view to the best interests of the corporation and must exercise the care, diligence, and skill that a reasonable, prudent person would exercise in comparable circumstances. In other words, when wearing the hat of a director, you must act as a reasonable person would in the same circumstances; therefore, you cannot hide behind the excuse that you were not aware of the circumstances, did not make reasonable inquiries about the problem, or simply chose to ignore it. If a court were to find that the reasonable approach in any particular situation would have been for you to have made certain necessary inquiries and you as a director did not do so, you would have some liability to the company and be subject to an action against you by either the company or the shareholders.

Besides this duty of care and skill, a director accepts the risk of personal liability toward the company. If you agree to an issuance of shares or a payment of dividends when the company is not in a financial position to do so, you as a director may be personally responsible to cover those losses.

Directors are also jointly and severally liable to employees of the corporation for all debts not exceeding six months' wages payable to each employee for services performed for the corporation.

Directors are personally responsible to Revenue Canada for employees' share of tax remittances that must be paid by all employees of a corporation. The one exception to this law is found in the Income Tax Act, section 227.1(3). A director who is not active in the day-to-day operation of the corporation, and who can prove that he or she exercised due diligence to prevent the failure to remit the tax will not be liable. This means that a director must take reasonable steps in order to satisfy himself or herself that the corporation had instituted proper procedures to pay these source deductions.

Two areas of concern have been created by new laws. Directors are jointly and severally liable for any GST not paid by a corporation. Defences similar to those referred to above are available. The second area of potential liability is environmental. Directors may be personally responsible for all environmental damages caused by any business carried on by a company to third parties.

Directors should also be aware that if they are at a meeting where resolutions are passed or actions are taken, they are deemed to have consented to the passing of each resolution unless they specifically request that their dissent be entered on the record. However, a director is not liable for personal damages if in good faith, he or she relies on opinions or information provided by professional advisors.

Because these standards are so high, it is a good idea to ensure that the company protects or indemnifies directors from liability. The corporation has the right to indemnify directors against any costs, charges, and expenses that they may be required to pay to settle an action or satisfy a judgment as long as the director acted in the best interests of the company. Sample #5 is an Acknowledgment and Indemnity Agreement, which should be entered into between each director and the company to provide for this type of indemnification. (An alternative method of protection that may be considered is directors' liability insurance; however, this is expensive.)

Because directors are in a position of trust, they must not act in any way that will create a conflict of interest or allow them to take unnecessary or unwarranted advantage of the company.

4. Officers — rights, duties, and liabilities

In the large, public corporation, the actual day-to-day operations of the company are carried out by corporate management or the executives of the company. Depending on the size of the company, this group could range from a handful of individuals to several thousand. They are appointed by the board of directors and are, therefore, employees of the company; depending on their position, they are given various responsibilities to handle.

The same situation will arise in your company. You will undoubtedly be called upon to perform many tasks on a day-to-day basis, whether it involves working to generate the revenue for the company, providing certain bookkeeping or secretarial services, or hiring others to handle various jobs.

The various officers of a company, like directors, have the same responsibilities and duties toward the company and the same standards of care that were discussed earlier.

Normally, in your capacity as an officer, you will be wearing the hat of a president or secretary, or both. There is really no magic in the title. It is not the title that determines what your duties are. There are some things that a president will normally always have authority to do, such as sign documents, etc., but the articles or the by-laws of the company will also give particular officers responsibility for certain functions and duties.

For your company, you will normally designate yourself as the president, and if it is a one-person company, you can be designated as president-secretary. If there are two shareholders involved, then each should be provided with a title. This gives them credibility in dealing with other companies and lending institutions and is useful for paying officers' salaries, income-splitting, and other tax-saving devices.

Officers are subject to the authority of the board of directors. The board has the power to hire and fire officers. Shareholders cannot remove the officers, except through their voting control over the election of the board.

5. Employee/creditor

In addition to the hats of shareholder, director, and officer, it is quite likely that you will be employed by the company in some capacity, and will, therefore, wear the hat of an employee. As an employee, you are contractually bound to the company. Normally, these contracts are not written. If you are hiring an employee for less than one year, the employment contract is legally enforceable even though it is not in writing.

In an attempt to avoid, or at least defer, the payment of income tax to Revenue Canada, some people set up private companies and hire themselves out to those companies as consultants. In this way, you, as the consultant, are not required to pay certain tax remittances on receipt of monies from the company and can therefore defer payment of a portion of your taxes for some period of time.

SAMPLE #5
ACKNOWLEDGMENT AND INDEMNITY AGREEMENT

ACKNOWLEDGMENT & INDEMNITY AGREEMENT

WHEREAS SLIM, TRIM and WHIM, (hereinafter collectively called the "Shareholders") are the registered owners of the "Corporation") set forth opposite each such Party in Schedule "A" attached hereto;

AND WHEREAS ATLAS SHRUG of the City of Calgary, in the Province of Alberta, (hereinafter called the "Director") has agreed to serve as a Director (and Officer) of the Corporation at the request of the Shareholders and in consideration of the execution and delivery of the within Agreement by the Shareholders;

AND WHEREAS the Director has no financial interest in the Corporation nor is the Director a beneficial Shareholder of the Corporation;

AND WHEREAS the Shareholders, acting under authority contained in the Alberta Business Corporations Act, have agreed to enter into a Unanimous Shareholders Agreement which restricts, to the extent set forth therein, the rights, powers and discretion of the Directors of the Corporation to manage the business and affairs of the Corporation.

NOW THEREFORE THIS INDENTURE WITNESSETH as follows:

1.   The Director hereby acknowledges that he has actual notice of the terms of the Unanimous Shareholders Agreement made amongst the Shareholders and the Corporation dated the 1st day of May, 199-.

2.   The undersigned Shareholders, for themselves, their respective heirs, executors, administrators, successors and assigns, hereby jointly and severally agree to indemnify and save harmless the Director, and his heirs, executors, administrators, successors and assigns of and from all costs, charges, losses, expenses and claims whatsoever arising out of or in any way incidental to the Director holding or having held office as a Director while acting or purporting to act in that capacity or by reason of any breach by the Shareholders of the rights, powers, duties and liabilities expressed in the Unanimous Shareholders' Agreement to be assumed by the Shareholders.

3.   The undersigned Shareholders further agree that the indemnity granted hereinbefore to the Director shall extend to all costs, charges, expenses or claims that arise or occur through the acts, receipts, neglects or defaults of any other director or officer of the Corporation, the insufficiency or deficiency of title to any property acquired by, for, or on behalf of the Corporation, or the insufficiency or deficiency of any security in or upon which any of the monies of the Corporation shall be invested, or any loss or damages arising from the bankruptcy, insolvency or wrongful act of any depository of the Corporation, or for any loss occasioned by any error of judgment or oversight on the part of the Director.

4.   Nothing herein shall relieve the Director from the duty to act in accordance with the Act and the regulations thereunder or from liability for any breach thereof.

5.   Wherever the singular and masculine or neuter are used throughout this Indemnity, they shall be construed as if the plural and feminine has been used where the context or the party or parties hereto so require, and the rest of the sentence shall be construed as if the necessary grammatical and terminological changes thereby rendered necessary had been made.

6.   This Agreement shall enure to the benefit of and be binding upon the undersigned, and their respective heirs, executors, administrators, successors and assigns.

      IN WITNESS WHEREOF the Parties have hereunto set their hands and seals, as of the 1st day of May, 199-.

SIGNED, SEALED AND DELIVERED in the
presence of:

_____
WITNESS

_____
SLIM-SHAREHOLDER

_____
WITNESS

_____
TRIM-SHAREHOLDER

_____
WITNESS

_____
WHIM-SHAREHOLDER

_____
WITNESS

_____
ATLAS SHRUG-DIRECTOR

18

This type of planning is perfectly legitimate as long as the consultant is really recognized as a consultant. As the old saying goes, "a rose by any other name is still a rose...." Revenue Canada will not treat you as a consultant simply because you call yourself one. They may still consider you to be an employee.

Although there are a number of distinguishing features between consultants and employees, the critical test is one of control. If the corporation can be seen to be in control of most aspects of the work done by the consultant including the nature of the work, hours of work, where the work is done, etc., there is a very good chance that you will be seen as an employee, and treated accordingly.

In order to ensure that you will be properly recognized as a consultant, a written agreement between you and the company, which emphasizes that control on all of the important matters relating to the work to be done rests with you as consultant, is necessary. It is then important to document the work done, hours spent on that particular project, and any other matter which may be of assistance in later dealing with Revenue Canada if this issue should ever arise. If you are at all concerned, Revenue Canada will issue you a ruling which will resolve the issue one way or the other.

You will also, in all likelihood, wear the hat of a creditor of the company, because you will be providing either the cash or assets of one type or another necessary to start the business. Therefore, if the company gets into financial difficulty, you as a creditor can take legal action against the company.

As a creditor, you have neither legal obligations nor duties of good faith toward the company. However, be advised that there are laws to prevent you from removing assets or monies from the company to pay your indebtedness which would have the effect of either making the company insolvent or giving you a "preference" over other creditors.

If your company gets into financial difficulty and the company is indebted to you, seek some professional advice about the best method of dealing with the repayment of all debts, including the one owed to you.

d. HOW DO I ACQUIRE AND HOLD MY INTEREST IN THE COMPANY?

1. Shares and share capital

The magic link between you and your company is through the shares that the company will issue to you. It is with share capital that the company acquires its solid financial base and provides for the control and management of the organization.

Again referring to the example of a large, public company, hundreds and perhaps thousands of individuals interested in investing in the stock market have the opportunity of acquiring shares of any one of thousands of companies listed on a number of stock exchanges in Alberta and around the world. Although it is unlikely that shareholders ever see the share certificates they buy, they are, in effect, acquiring a small slice of ownership and control in that company which is theirs to buy, sell, or retain.

Similarly, in your company, the shares that you receive will also provide you with a certain percentage of the control, management, and investment opportunity in your company.

Basically, a share is an asset. Like a dollar bill, it is a physical representation of quite a complex legal interest.

Under the Business Corporations Act, a share or share certificate is classified as a "negotiable instrument." Like a dollar bill, if the share certificate is in "street form" or signed off (i.e., it is signed on the back of the certificate), it can be passed validly from person to person as easily as currency is exchanged between parties.

It is, therefore, very important, if you want to restrict the transfer of your shares, to mark some type of notation on the share certificate indicating that the shares are "non-negotiable."

The term "authorized capital" is used to define the total number of shares that the company is allowed to issue. The term "issued share capital" is defined as the actual number of shares that the company has issued. These items are discussed in more detail in chapter 4.

You should note that each company is authorized to issue a certain number of shares (in some cases, the number will actually be an unlimited number of shares); those shares may then be sold by the company for cash or other valuable consideration, which is transferred to the company. The company is then able to utilize the cash or other assets to further its business interests.

This concept of equity participation is fundamental to corporate existence and is often the most practical way for a company to raise money.

2. Share rights

What rights do you obtain by owning shares in a company? The owner of a share company has three basic rights vis-à-vis his or her shares. Those three rights are the right to vote, the right to a dividend, and the right to participate in a percentage of the company's assets upon dissolution.

The right to vote is fundamental to corporate ownership; it is the way control is exercised. As noted earlier, this right to vote gives the shareholders the authority to set up the company in the way that they want and to elect directors and make other major decisions affecting the company.

Profits in a company are paid out to shareholders in the form of dividends. In the discussion of the financial aspects of the company in chapter 8, I will refer to and define the term "retained earnings," which includes both the profits generated by the business over the course of a year as well as the initial share investment. Dividends are paid out of retained earnings if and when they are approved by the board of directors.

For example, if there are 100 shares in the company and, at year end, the company has $1 000 remaining after payment of all current liabilities, the company may, by resolution of the board of directors, pay that money to its shareholders by declaring a dividend in the amount of $10 per share. All dividends must be paid out equally to shareholders owning the same class of shares. Therefore, if you desire, from a tax point of view or otherwise, to issue dividends to one shareholder and not another, different classes of shares will have to be issued. Please refer to the discussion in chapter 3 as to how that may be accomplished.

The third major right of a shareholder is the right to your piece of the corporate pie upon dissolution. This right relates back to the concept of limited liability and investment in a company. If there are 100 shares issued in a company and the company decides for one reason or another to dissolve, all of the expenses and liabilities of the company first have to be extinguished. Once that has been accomplished, any of the funds left in the company can be given out to the shareholders in a final distribution of funds. Therefore, if there is $100 000 left in the company, the shareholders will receive $1 000 for each share they held, despite the fact that they may have paid as low as 1¢ or $1 for the share.

Conversely, if after payment of all liabilities and expenses, there is only $50 left in the company, each shareholder will receive only 50¢ for each share held in the company even though they may have initially paid far in excess of 50¢ for each share. However, under the concept of limited liability, shareholders put their initial share purchase price at risk, and if business is bad, could lose up to 100% of the initial share investment — but can lose nothing more.

The three rights just discussed basically define what are generally referred to as the rights associated with "common shares." These shares are to be distinguished from "preferred shares" which, by definition, contain some form of preference over the common shares. A more detailed explanation of this distinction is explained later in this chapter.

3. Classes of shares

(a) Par value and no par value

Prior to discussing how and why different classes of shares may be issued, let us discuss the sometimes confusing concept of par value and no par value shares. Thankfully, under the Business Corporations Act, par value shares have been abolished and no shares may now be issued with a par value.

What this means for your company is that shares can be issued and sold by the company at whatever price the board of directors deems satisfactory. What normally happens, of course, is that the initial incorporators of the company will acquire the shares at a very low price, normally $1 per share or less.

As the company prospers and other individuals become interested in getting in on the action, the company can issue new shares to them, likely at a higher price. Similarly, existing shareholders can sell their own shares to other individuals at a higher price and incur a profit, which is normally characterized by law as a capital gain.

Shares no longer carry the nomenclature of "$1 par value" or "$10 par value" because those numbers simply confuse the issue and really do not define what the share is worth at any given time.

The actual share value is determined in one way only and that is simply by dividing the number of shares into the retained earnings (the value of the company's assets less its liabilities) of the company using the following formula:

$$\text{Share value} = \frac{\text{Retained earnings}}{\text{Total number of shares}}$$

This is an important formula because it illustrates to you what happens to the value of your shares when new shares are issued. For example, assume that you acquire 100 shares and pay $100 for them when initially setting up your business. Before any other assets go into the company besides the $100, your shares are obviously worth $1 a piece. If you let Frank Funds into the company, however, and allow him to acquire 100 shares with an investment of $50, then by using the formula, the value of your shares will have been diluted from $1 per share to 75¢, even though at that point you may have put more money in for your shares. Please note that this is perfectly legal, but not particularly brilliant from your point of view, unless there is a good business reason for allowing your friend into the company. Perhaps the expertise that Frank can provide to the business will make it worthwhile for you to make this sacrifice.

As time goes on, you hope the retained earnings in the company will increase and your share values will go up. Let us now assume that after one year's operation, your retained earnings have grown from $100 to $10 000 and there are still only 100 shares issued, all of which you hold. Using the formula, your shares are worth $100 each, despite the fact that you paid only $1 for them.

If you want to bring in new investment capital and still maintain your share value at $100 per share, you will have to ensure that the company issues shares at no less a price than $100 per share. You could also sell your own shares in the company to the investor. The effect of that would be that the issued capital of the company will remain at 100 shares and, therefore, as far as the book value of the share is concerned it will remain at $100 per share no matter what price you sell it for to the third party. A third party, however, would probably not pay more than $100 for that share unless there is a great expectation that the share value will increase because of an increase in retained earnings or because you have increased the value of the business by creating something known as "good will." Good will is normally defined as the intangible asset that a business creates due to its reputation and good name.

Do not think that you can simply issue shares to yourself and declare large dividends or sell shares at high prices. Certain safeguards have been written into the legislation. Under the Business Corporations Act, directors have personal liability if they declare dividends in such a manner that after the dividend monies are paid, the company is unable to meet its financial responsibilities or is deemed to be insolvent.

Accordingly, check with your accountant or bookkeeper prior to issuing dividends to make sure that you will not have any personal responsibility to make up the debts of the company if the company is short on cash.

(b) Common and preferred shares

As we discussed above, a common share has three basic rights. In many situations, it is desirable to issue more than one class of shares. It may be that an investor coming into the company will want some form of preference or priority in receiving dividends if he or she is going to put money in.

Alternatively, you may wish to have another class of shares that you can issue to your spouse in order to split income by issuing dividends to either of you, if and when required.

In fact, there are many reasons why more than one class of shares may be necessary, and the Business Corporations Act allows a company to create as many different classes of shares as desired. The only requirement under the Business Corporations Act is that at least one class of shares contain the three rights discussed above and that if a company has only one class of shares, then those three rights must attach to each share and each of the shares must be equal in every respect.

If the corporation is going to have different classes of shares, they must be designated as Class A shares, Class B shares, etc.

The "preference" that is usually attached to shares is a preference for the payment of dividends or rights associated with voting or non-voting; however, the preference may be for any number of rights. Preference shares are particularly useful for transferring assets to the company and for other tax savings plans available to companies.

As you can now see, the great flexibility in setting up a company is founded in its share structure. The use of different types or "classes" of shares can provide many different ways that a company can pay out profits to shareholders in order to minimize taxes. The question of control of the company is determined by who is entitled to the voting and non-voting shares.

Capital for the company can be raised by luring investors into the company with the promise of receiving a preference or priority to dividends in their shares as compared to the shares held by the common shareholders. In fact, many of the shares currently for sale on the stock market are preferred shares, which have a preference as to dividends, etc.

There are a number of rights and qualifications that may be attached to shares. You may have heard of shares that are referred to with fancy terms known as cumulative shares, redeemable shares, shares with a redemption value, etc.; these terms refer to various rights that can be attached to shares and are designed either for tax avoidance purposes or to provide some form of preference to potential investors. For purposes of the type of company that you will be incorporating, however, these types of shares will probably not be necessary.

It is not an exaggeration to refer to a company's share structure as the building block upon which it is built.

(c) Stated capital account

Under the Business Corporations Act, your corporation must maintain a separate capital account for each class of shares it issues. The shares, when they are issued, must be fully paid for and whatever cash or cash equivalent value is received by the company for those shares must be accounted for in a separate account for each class of shares issued.

The stated capital per share of any class of shares basically relates back to the formula discussed earlier. The company is entitled to buy back shares of a corporation but in doing so the necessary reduction to the capital account must be made. For assistance in setting up these accounts, consult your accountant or bookkeeper.

Here is a simple example of how the stated capital account is maintained. If a company initially issues 100 shares at a price of $1 per share, the stated capital immediately after that transaction is $100. If, six minutes later, the company sells another 100 shares at $2 per share, the new stated capital of the company will rise to $300. The average price per share has now become $1.50 per share.

e. WHAT TYPE OF COMPANY DO I WANT?

1. Classification of companies

Under the old Alberta Companies Act, companies were classified as either "private" or "public" companies. The act was initially designed so that large companies that had many shareholders and traded actively on the open market would be public companies and small family companies would be private companies with many fewer reporting requirements.

This plan did not work well because many of the large companies maintained their status as private companies, and the necessary information that should have been available to shareholders and others was simply not required. However, the legislators did want to maintain some form of classification system in the Business Corporations Act to allow smaller companies to operate with minimal governmental interference. Therefore, the Business Corporations Act divides companies into three groups.

(a) Non-distributing corporations with 15 or fewer shareholders

This company is similar to the old private company and is designed to accommodate the vast majority of companies that will be incorporated. The rest of the book is about this kind of company. It is subject to the least amount of regulation, but certain forms still must be filed with the provincial government. By definition, the company is restricted to 15 or fewer shareholders and cannot distribute or sell shares to the public.

(b) Non-distributing corporations with more than 15 shareholders

This company has greater public disclosure and filing requirements and by definition can have more than 15 shareholders. However, it must be a non-distributing company and cannot sell shares to the public.

(c) Distributing company

This type of company is comparable to what in the past was called a public company. It is saddled with a number of public disclosure requirements as well as additional checks and balances imposed by the Business Corporations Act. However, this company is allowed, after it complies with all necessary corporate and securities laws, to sell shares to the public.

As stated above, the type of company that you will be incorporating will in all likelihood be a non-distributing company with fewer than 15 shareholders. I will be referring to that type of company throughout this book as a non-distributing company. Please realize, however, that if you want to have more than 15 shareholders in your company, you will then be incorporating a slightly different type of company and will have certain additional disclosure and filing requirements.

2. Companies not subject to the Business Corporations Act

The Business Corporations Act does not contain any provisions regarding the incorporation of non-profit corporations. Therefore, any person interested in establishing a society or association for purposes other than a profit-oriented business should set it up either pursuant to the requirements of the Societies Act, which is another Alberta statute, or under part 9 of the old Companies Act, which provides for non-profit companies and will continue in force pending the enactment of new legislation.

As will be discussed briefly in chapter 3, professional corporations may be incorporated under the Business Corporations Act, subject to compliance with legislation governing the profession in question.

The old Companies Act also provided for certain very specialized types of companies known as "companies limited by guarantee" or "specially limited companies." Neither of these types of companies are allowed under the Business Corporations Act.

f. HOW DO I GET MY COMPANY NAME?

1. Guidelines for selecting corporate names

Of all of the considerations necessary in setting up a company, the one that seems to provide the most enjoyment and the most frustration is the selection of a company name. With so many companies being incorporated both federally and provincially, obtaining a name that is not in conflict with an existing corporation has become more and more difficult. In fact, in many cases, it can become downright impossible.

Under the Business Corporations Act, a new procedure for the reservation of names has been introduced. However, the actual guidelines regarding the selection of a name have not changed. The only difference is that the administrators now share with us the criteria they utilize in selecting names.

Because name search organizations charge approximately $50 each time you wish to check out or reserve a name, it is going to become more and more important that the names you submit for approval can be approved. I will, therefore, attempt to briefly outline the requirements in current use for selecting a name. Remember, however, that the final determination will always be at the Registrar's discretion. Even when a name has been reserved for you, the Registrar may not accept it or the name may be challenged by another company with a similar name. The following items are given only as guidelines.

A company name basically contains three elements:

(a) The distinctive element

(b) The descriptive element

(c) The legal element

The distinctive element in a corporate name is that part of the name that is the unique identifier of the name of the company. This element is necessary to distinguish your company name from anybody else who is carrying on business in the same general area and whose descriptive element is the same.

To be approved, this portion of the name must be distinctive from any other name used in any other Alberta company. It can be a combination of letters, a combination of words, or simply a distinctive adjective or noun that will set your company apart from all others.

For example, if you are going into the manufacturing business, you would not be allowed to incorporate the name "Manufacturing Ltd." That name lacks a distinctive element and would be seen as an attempt to corner the market in names dealing with the manufacturing business. Although this may be desirable from your point of view, it is not desirable from the point of view of all others who may someday get involved in similar businesses. Your name will, therefore, be refused.

However, if you add a distinctive element to the name, such as "Joe's," "ABC," or "Foothills," then, unless there is another company in existence that uses any of those distinctive elements or has a name that closely resembles the distinctive element that you require, your name will be approved.

This portion of the corporate name is usually the most difficult to create and to have approved. Be creative. Do not use words like Alberta, Calgary, Edmonton, Western, etc. because most have been used previously.

If you have come up with a name that you really must use, but it is not approved, remember that you can always use that name as a trade name as long as you register it and do not include the legal element in the name. There is no need to have a name approved prior to filing a trade name declaration, but you are, of course, subject to legal action by someone already using a similar name.

The descriptive element normally describes a corporation's main business. Those words include such things as Investments, Manufacturing, Sales, etc.

Many companies incorporated for investment purposes have attempted to use, as the descriptive portion of the name, words such as Investments, Holdings, or Enterprises. My experience with the Companies Branch is that these names are less and less likely to be available simply because they do not, in many instances, describe the corporation's main business. So be slightly more creative in coming up with a descriptive element in order to ensure that your name will be approved.

For companies engaged in active businesses, words such as Marketing, Sales, Design, Manufacturing, etc., are usually approved without any problem.

The legal element of a company name can include, in addition to the word Limited or Ltd., the words Incorporated, Inc., Corporation or Corp. The reason for inclusion of the legal element is to warn members of the public that they are dealing with entities having limited liability and, therefore, they will not have any personal recourse against the particular individual they are dealing with.

The use of the legal element of a name is absolutely essential; the only exception is in the use of a professional corporation where the legal element is deemed by the law to be the words "Professional Corporation."

The Companies Branch has issued regulations that itemize what names will not be approved. To summarize those regulations, the following names are restricted under the Business Corporations Act:

(a) Names that use the word Royal or imply that the company is carrying on business under royal or government patronage, approval, or authority

(b) Names that denote that the corporation is sponsored or controlled or affiliated with a university or professional association

(c) Names that imply or denote that the company carries on the business of a bank, loan company, insurance company, trust company, financial intermediary, or stock exchange (unless the necessary government consents are obtained)

(d) Names containing obscene words or phrases that are scandalous, obscene, or immoral

(e) Names that are not distinctive because they are too general and descriptive only of goods or services to be dealt in, or primarily give only the name of an individual or a geographic name, i.e., National Manufacturing Ltd., DMG Ltd., etc.

(f) Names that could be confused with existing corporate names and trade marks or trade names

(g) Names that are similar to the name of a company or corporation already incorporated in Alberta or federally

(h) Names which in any way refer to the Canadian Olympic Association, Kananaskis and/or Nakiska, or the Alberta Heritage Savings Trust Fund

Despite these prohibitions, there are exceptions for some names. At the discretion of the Registrar, the following kinds of names will be approved:

(a) Names that could be confused with the name of an existing company if that company has not carried on business for the preceding two years, has consented to the use of the name, and undertakes to either dissolve or change its name

(b) Names that do contain a word similar to a word contained in a name with a trade mark or trade name if the owner of the trade mark or trade name has consented and the new corporate name is not confusing when compared with the trade mark or trade name

(c) Names that may be confused with the name of an old corporation provided that the new corporation is a successor of the old corporation. The old corporation must dissolve within six months and the new corporation must include as part of its corporate name the year it was incorporated, e.g., Joe's Manufacturing (1997) Ltd.

If this all seems too confusing or frustrating for you, you will be pleased to learn that you can incorporate a company with a number with no problem whatsoever. Your company name will then be "123456" Alberta Ltd., which will be as valid a name as any other name that can be approved. You can keep that name and operate under a trade name, which can be filed at the Corporate Registry so that you can have the best of both worlds. As well, by special resolution, the company can at any time change to a more desirable or acceptable name, although this will cost the company approximately $75 in registration costs, plus the name search fee.

Many times, people get frustrated with this name game and quickly get the feeling that if this is the way it's going to be in terms of the bureaucracy and paperwork, maybe a company isn't really worth it. But the name reservation process is sometimes the most difficult part of incorporating; and you can circumvent many of these initial problems if you are anxious to get into business immediately by using a number company with a registered trade name. That will get you in business right away, and you can then worry about the change of name at your leisure.

2. The name reservation procedure

As noted above, there is now a charge for every name that is sent in for approval. Names must be submitted to private name search companies that use a complex computer data bank (known as the NUANS system) to search, examine, and recommend potential names. These search companies will provide you with an extensive, written search report that lists the proposed name plus an extended list of existing provincial and federal names, as well as registered trade marks that are in any way similar to your proposed name.

Sample #6 shows a sample NUANS report and name reservation.

This report must be submitted for approval with the other incorporation documents to the Registrar's office. A complete list of private search companies may be found in your local telephone directory.

If the name is approved, it will then be reserved for you for a period of 90 days during which time you will have a priority to the use of that name. If you are willing to pay an additional fee, you are entitled to an extension of 90 days if you have not incorporated at the end of the first period. By the end of the extension period, if you have not incorporated, you will lose your priority to that name and will have to reapply.

A complete list of all corporate names, which is updated once a month, is available on microfiche. This list will also show the date of incorporation and the date a company was struck off (if it has been struck off). Under the Business Corporations Act, if a company has been struck off the register for three years, its name is then available to others. If you can look at this list, you will have a great advantage in determining what names are available. It is available for viewing in Companies Branch offices in Calgary and Edmonton.

The Business Corporations Act does provide for a procedure that allows you to appeal a decision of the Registrar. You might want to appeal either when the Registrar has turned your name down or when you want the Registrar to force another company to change its name because the name may confuse the public and therefore affect your business. As this area may require a trip to court, legal advice should be obtained.

The private search houses now have the exclusive right to obtain name approvals. Subject to unusual circumstances, you can get a name reservation in 24 hours. Under the system, it is relatively easy to get a new name approved. The real risk to a corporation is that it might have to change its name

after it is established in business if a controversy arises.

There is no charge and no need to reserve for a numbered company. Under the Business Corporations Act, the name of the numbered company can be changed by special resolution (see chapter 5). As well, there is currently no requirement for the Registrar to publish this form of change of name in the *Alberta Gazette.*

g. PRE-INCORPORATION CONTRACTS

The Alberta Business Corporations Act allows for "pre-incorporation contracts." These are contracts or agreements that are entered into by the incorporators with third parties, for example, to lease space, acquire stationery, or purchase office furniture before the company is actually incorporated.

If the company, after it is incorporated, ratifies and confirms a pre-incorporation contract, that contract becomes legally binding on the company. The incorporators then will no longer have any personal liability to the third party.

This ratification should be done in a directors' resolution. It is also important for the incorporators to make sure that the third party knows that he or she is making this contract on behalf of a company to be incorporated at the time the pre-incorporation contract or agreement is made; otherwise, the third party may have the right to sue the incorporator personally.

h. CONCLUSION

I hope you have now acquired a brief understanding of the world of business incorporation. The next chapter moves into a detailed discussion of the actual incorporation procedure. The many and varied considerations discussed in this chapter will be translated in the next chapter into very important, practical steps to take when setting up a corporation.

SAMPLE #6
NUANS REPORT

NUANS™REPORT   RAPPORT NUAN

CDA CANADA, NUANS-ALBERTA   CORPORATIONS   AACCUCA CXA 4881

                    ? C. & P. GIANNA RESTAURANTS   PAGE 2/6
      20070303 ALBERTA   LTD   85/ 8/ 9

     20 19235 ALTA 56 116 FOOD GIANT MARKETS LTD
        AMALG   INACTV   81/ 8/14

      1380583 CDA   THE DRUGSTORE GIANT INC
        URBAN MONTREA QUE   H4Z1E4   82/10/26
     72
      1191233 CDA   RESTAURANT PAPA GINO INC
        MONTREAL   QUE   H2N2B7   81/ 8/20
     74
     20 99315 ALTA   GIAN-CARL WELDESIGN LTD
     EDMONTON, ALB.T5T1B4 ABCORP   77/ 1/26

      1380583 CDA   LE GEANT DE LA PHARMACIE INC
        URBAN MONTREA QUE   H4Z1E4   82/10/26

       286460 CDA   LES ENTREPRISES GIANNANGELO INC
        ANJOU   QUE   H1K2V2   78/ 3/17
     72
     20 79433 ALTA   THE MAGIC PAN RESTAURANTS LTD
        CHNGED   INACTV   75/10/ 6
     73
      1152041 CDA   ANDREAS GIANNAKIS HOLDINGS INC
        URBAN MONTREA QUE   81/ 6/ 4
     72
     20 74819 ALTA   CFI RESTAURANTS INC
     EDMONTON, ALB.T5J1V3 ABCORP   NU830408   74/ 8/ 8

     20299224 ALTA   CFI RESTAURANTS (CONFEDERATION) INC
     EDMONTON, ALT.T5J1V3 ABCORP   NU830929   83/ 5/31
     73
     21 6467 N-AL 62 716 GIANT DISCOUNT FOODS LIMITED
        STRUCK   INACTV   REG.ALTA   71/ 6/15
     72
     20 71145 ALTA 74 214 BABY GIANT MARTS LTD
        STRUCK   INACTV   81/ 7/31

     20 19235 ALTA   FOOD TOWN LTD
        CHNGED   INACTV   58/ 9/27
     71
     20271122 ALTA   GINZA RESTAURANT LTD
     CALGARY, ALBE.T2A6K4 ABCORP   81/ 5/ 8

     20285291 ALTA   CIPRIANOS PIZZA & RESTAURANT LTD
     CALGARY, ALBE.T2P1G1 ABCORP   82/ 6/30

     20203559 ALTA   PISA ITALIAN RESTAURANT LTD
     RED DEER, ALB.T4N6M4 ABCORP   79/ 3/ 5

       95087 CDA   TRAN CHAU VIETNAM RESTAURANTS LTD
        OTTAWA   ONT   PEN-FUND   79/12/11

28

3
STEP-BY-STEP INCORPORATION PROCEDURES

This chapter will cover in detail the steps involved in actually incorporating your company.

At the outset you should be aware that the incorporation of a company does involve costs even if you do it without the help of a lawyer.

Under the Business Corporations Act, the government incorporation fee is now $300. See Appendix 2 for a detailed fee schedule outlining the costs of various filings with the Companies Branch. This registration fee is in addition to the name reservation fee discussed earlier.

You are also advised to purchase a prepared minute book with the necessary dividers, or at least acquire a binder and some dividers so that you can organize the company documents properly.

Samples of the documents are sprinkled throughout this chapter, and most are available either from the Companies Branch or from the publisher of this book (see the front of this book). Wherever possible, step-by-step instructions will be provided to assist you in filling out the documents. Appendix 1 provides a handy checklist of the procedures involved in incorporating your company.

a. NAME APPROVAL

I will assume that at this point you have already received approval for a name or you want to incorporate a number company.

If you submit documents for incorporation without having had the name approval in the hope that you can avoid the procedure, it will probably not save you any time. The full name reservation procedure will have to be followed before the examiners will do any work on the balance of your documents. This, however, does not apply for number companies.

If you have been carrying on business as a partnership or sole proprietorship, you should prepare a consent of your partnership or sole proprietorship in favor of the corporation to use the name that has been approved. This is simply to prevent anyone else from using the trade name that you used in your previous business structure. A partnership consent to use a similar name is shown in Sample #7.

b. THE ARTICLES OF INCORPORATION

The Articles of Incorporation form is the basic constitutional document for your company. The Articles set out the fundamental items that you have selected to use for your company. Under the Business Corporations Act it is Form 1.

This form must be submitted in duplicate to the Registrar of Companies with all the necessary information filled in. I will explain the document on a clause by clause basis, using as an example a fictitious person I shall call Stew Cooke. Mr. Cooke wants to open a restaurant in one of Calgary's new high-rise buildings. He had been carrying on a sole proprietorship and then brought his wife into partnership with him in a small restaurant in the suburbs. Now he has decided to take the big gamble and move into a downtown restaurant.

He has chosen the name of Skywalk Restaurant Ltd. and has had in writing an approval of the name. He is now at the point of filling in the incorporation documents. I will use his forms as a launching pad for a discussion about the information to be included in the form.

Let us now review Form 1 — the Articles of Incorporation — on a clause by clause basis. A completed Form 1 is shown in Sample #8.

Clause 1 — Name of corporation

Simply write in the approved name of the corporation as shown on the NUANS report. Be sure that the spelling is correct and that the legal portion of the name (the word Limited, Ltd., Incorporated, or Co.) is either spelled out in full or abbreviated depending on your preference. If you want to set up a number company, simply write or type in " " Alberta Ltd.

Clause 2 — Classes and shares

You already know that it is essential that a company have at least one class of common shares containing the three basic rights discussed in chapter 2. In order to provide more flexibility, more classes of shares can be created, although depending on the size of the company, it may not be necessary to create several classes of shares.

In past years, registration fees were based on the maximum number of shares that the corporation was authorized to issue. That is why most older companies used 20 000 as the maximum number of shares; 20 000 was the minimum number of shares people could get away with in terms of filing fees. However, that has changed. The fees are now the same no matter how many shares are authorized. It is, in fact, possible to incorporate a company with an unlimited number of authorized shares.

However, because the number of shares is really not as significant as the value of those shares, Mr. Cooke will include a maximum number of shares in his Articles of Incorporation.

Mr. Cooke wants to issue shares to his wife and to a third party who wishes to invest some money into the business, so it is a good idea to have more than one class of shares, especially since Mr. Cooke still wants to maintain control of the restaurant, even though he is prepared to share some of the profit with both his wife and the investor.

Accordingly, three classes of shares will be set up, to be known as Class A shares, Class B shares, and Class E preferred shares. (Class C and D shares are also available if they need to be issued later.)

The Class A shares will contain the three basic rights that shares are given: the right to vote, the right to a dividend, and the right to share in the corporate assets upon the dissolution of the company. These shares will be issued to Mr. Cooke.

The Class B shares will be similar to the Class A shares in every respect except that they will be non-voting shares. The B shares will be issued to Mr. Cooke's wife. She will then have the right to receive some of the profits of the company, which will allow income splitting between her and Mr. Cooke. But she will not have any say in the management of the restaurant, which does not interest her.

The holder of the Class E preferred shares will be entitled to receive a dividend in priority to the Class A or B shares whenever a dividend is declared by the board of directors. That dividend will be based on a 12% return on the investor's money and will be a cumulative dividend, that is, if a dividend is not declared in year one, then the amount of the dividend will carry over until year two, and so on. These shares will be issued to Mr. Cooke's investor.

By examining Sample #8, you will see that you can issue an unlimited number of shares of each class. That does not mean that you have to issue millions of shares, but you can if you want to!

CONSENT

SKYWALK RESTAURANT hereby consents to the use of the name SKYWALK RESTAU-RANT LTD.

In witness whereof the partners of SKYWALK RESTAURANT have hereunto affixed their signature.

DATED at the City of Calgary, in the Province of Alberta, this 15th day of April, 199-.

Stew Cooke

STEW COOKE

Carmel Cooke

CARMEL COOKE

Clause 3 — Restrictions, if any, on share transfer

Under the old Companies Act, a private company was required to include some form of restriction on the transfer of shares from one person to another. In other words, the shares could not be freely transferable from one party to another without some restriction on the company, which normally included such things as obtaining the consent of the board of directors.

In order to qualify your company as a non-distributing company, some form of restriction on the share transfers should still be included. In Mr. Cooke's company, the restriction is simply that no shares can be transferred without the consent of a majority of the board of directors.

Also included are two other restrictions that are normally found in most small companies. These restrictions are a restriction on the sale of shares to members of the public and a restriction on the number of shareholders to a maximum of 15 shareholders at any one time.

Another type of restriction that is now available is the pre-emptive right, which requires any shareholder who wants to sell shares to offer the shares for sale to all existing shareholders prior to selling them to any outside third parties.

Actually, the restrictions are limited only by your imagination, but they should not be so onerous that they will unduly restrict the ability to carry on business.

Any restrictions that are included on the transfer of shares will have to be clearly identified on the actual share certificate.

SAMPLE #8
ARTICLES OF INCORPORATION

IMPORTANT: PLEASE READ INSTRUCTIONS ON THE BACK OF THIS FORM

BUSINESS CORPORATIONS ACT
(SECTION 6)

FORM 1

 CONSUMER AND CORPORATE AFFAIRS

ARTICLES OF INCORPORATION

1. NAME OF CORPORATION:

SKYWALK RESTAURANT LTD.

2. THE CLASSES, AND ANY MAXIMUM NUMBER OF SHARES THAT THE CORPORATION IS AUTHORIZED TO ISSUE:

PLEASE SEE SCHEDULE "A" ATTACHED

3. RESTRICTIONS ON SHARE TRANSFERS (IF ANY):

(a)   No shares shall be transferred without the approval of the Board of Directors.

(b)   No shareholder may sell or transfer shares to members of the public.

(c)   There shall be, at all times, no more than fifteen (15) shareholders of the Company.

4. NUMBER, OR MINIMUM AND MAXIMUM NUMBER, OF DIRECTORS THAT THE CORPORATION MAY HAVE:

There shall be a minimum of one (1) and a maximum of three (3) directors.

5. IF THE CORPORATION IS RESTRICTED FROM CARRYING ON A CERTAIN BUSINESS, OR RESTRICTED TO CARRYING ON A CERTAIN BUSINESS, SPECIFY THE RESTRICTION(S):

None.

6. OTHER RULES OR PROVISIONS (IF ANY):

PLEASE SEE SCHEDULE "B" ATTACHED

7. DATE:

9-	05	19
YEAR	MONTH	DAY

INCORPORATORS NAMES:	ADDRESS (INCLUDING POSTAL CODE)	SIGNATURE
Stew Cooke	112 Eat Hardy Drive, S.W. Calgary, Alberta	*Stew Cooke*

FOR DEPARTMENTAL USE ONLY

INCORPORATION DATE

CCA-06.101
(Rev. 05/90)

THIS IS SCHEDULE "A" TO THE ARTICLES OF INCORPORATION OF
SKYWALK RESTAURANT LTD.

2. THE CLASSES AND ANY MAXIMUM NUMBER OF SHARES THAT THE
CORPORATION IS AUTHORIZED TO ISSUE.

The authorized capital of the Corporation shall be unlimited.

The Corporation is empowered to create, alter, vary, or delete classes of shares (each with or without an unlimited maximum consideration) as may from time to time be authorized by the Directors to the extent permitted by law.

Until further resolution of the Directors, the following classes of shares shall exist:

(a) An unlimited number of Class "A" voting shares without nominal or par value which may be issued and allotted by the Corporation from time to time for such consideration as may be paid from time to time, by resolution of the Directors of the Corporation.

(b) An unlimited number of Class "B" shares without nominal or par value which do not carry any voting rights whatsoever, and which may be issued and allotted by the Corporation from time to time for such consideration as may be paid from time to time, by resolution of the Directors of the Corporation.

(c) An unlimited number of Class "C" shares without nominal or par value which do not carry any voting rights whatsoever, and which may be issued and allotted by the Corporation from time to time for such consideration as may be paid from time to time, by resolution of the Directors of the Corporation.

(d) An unlimited number of Class "D" shares without nominal or par value which do not carry any voting rights whatsoever, and which may be issued and allotted by the Corporation from time to time for such consideration as may be paid from time to time, by resolution of the Directors of the Corporation.

(e) An unlimited number of Class "E" shares without nominal or par value which may be issued and allotted by the Corporation from time to time, by resolution of the Directors of the Corporation and which shall bear the following rights:

   (i) The shares may be redeemed by the Corporation or retracted by the Shareholder at such time and at a premium set by the Corporation by resolution of the Directors at the time the shares are first issued;

   (ii) The Corporation may, by resolution of the Directors, buy back the shares at the lowest price at which, in the opinion of the Directors of the Corporation, such shares are obtainable but not exceeding an amount per share equal to the premium for redemption set by the Corporation at the time the shares were first issued;

   (iii) The shares will bear a fixed preferential non-cumulative cash dividend in a percentage (per annum) of the redemption amount to be set by the Corporation by resolution of the Directors at the time the shares were first issued;

   (iv) The shares will be entitled to a prior return on liquidation or winding up in an amount equal to the premium set when the shares were first issued;

(v)　The shares will be non-participating in profits except to the extent of the premium on redemption, retraction, buy-back, liquidation, or winding up as herein defined;

(vi)　The shares shall have such voting rights as may be approved by the Directors at the time of the first issuance of this class of shares.

Note: Each class of shares created by the Board of Directors carries with it the distinction and right to receive dividends exclusive of other classes of shares in the Corporation; the determination of all matters relating to which class or classes of shares shall receive dividends shall be determined solely and exclusively by the Board of Directors of the Corporation in accordance with applicable law.

THIS IS SCHEDULE "B" TO THE ARTICLES OF INCORPORATION OF
SKYWALK RESTAURANT LTD.

6.   OTHER PROVISIONS.

(a) A Shareholder or any other person entitled to attend a meeting of Shareholders may participate in the meeting by means of telephone or other telecommunication facilities that permit all persons participating in the meeting to hear each other (if all the Shareholders entitled to vote at the meeting consent) and a person participating in such a meeting by those means is deemed to be present at the meeting.

(b) If all the Directors of the Corporation consent, a Director may participate in a meeting of the Directors or a committee of the Directors by means of such telephone or other telecommunication facilities that permit all persons participating in the meeting to hear each other and a Director participating in such a meeting by those means is deemed to be present at the meeting. Any such consent shall be effective whether given before or after the meeting to which it relates and may be given with respect to all meetings of the Directors and of committees of the Directors.

(c) The Directors may from time to time on behalf of the Corporation without authorization of the Shareholders:

(i)   borrow money upon the credit of the Corporation;

(ii)   issue, re-issue, sell or pledge bonds, debentures, notes or other evidences of indebtedness or guarantee of the Corporation whether secured or unsecured;

(iii) to the extent permitted by law, raise and assist in raising money for, by way of bonus, loan, promise, endorsement, guarantee or otherwise any person or Corporation, whether or not the Corporation has business relations with that person or Corporation, and guarantee the performance or fulfillment of any contracts or obligations of any such person or Corporation, and in particular, guarantee the payment of the principal of an interest in securities, mortgages and liabilities of any such person or Corporation;

(iv) mortgage, hypothecate, pledge or otherwise create a security interest in all or any currently owned or subsequently acquired real or personal, moveable or immoveable property of the Corporation including book debts, rights, powers, franchises and undertakings, to secure any such bonds, debentures, notes or other evidences of indebtedness or guarantee or any other present or future indebtedness, liability or obligation of the Corporation.

Nothing in this section limits or restricts the borrowing of money by the Corporation on bills of exchange or promissory notes made, drawn, accepted, or endorsed by or on behalf of the Corporation.

(v)   delegate the powers contained in this Article to such officers or directors of the Corporation and to such extent and in such manner as may be set out in the By-laws;

(vi) lend to or guarantee, with or without security, the contracts of any person of the Corporation, wheresoever incorporated, having dealings or business relations with the Corporation or with whom the Corporation proposes to have dealings or business relations, and the contracts of any person or Corporation proposing to buy or own shares of capital stock of the Corporation securing or evidencing an obligation in respect of the purchase price of such shares, or otherwise.

(d) The Directors may, by resolution, make, amend, or repeal any By-laws that regulate the business or affairs of the Corporation.

(e) A resolution in writing either ordinary or special signed by all the Shareholders entitled to vote on that resolution at a meeting of Shareholders is as valid as if it had been passed at a meeting of the Shareholders.

(f) A resolution in writing either ordinary or special signed by all the Directors entitled to vote on that resolution at a meeting of the Directors or a committee of Directors, if any, is as valid as if it had been passed at a meeting of the Directors or the committee of Directors if any.

(g) The Directors may, in their sole discretion, treat Shareholders of any separate class of shares differently for the purpose of dividends and may declare dividends on any class or classes without declaring any dividend on any other classes and may declare dividends on all classes at different times or at the same time in different amounts for each class or provide that same may be payable at different times.

Clause 4 — Number (or minimum and maximum number) of directors

The role of directors has already been discussed. They basically serve as the management arm of the company through a Board of Directors. In most small companies, the directors are the same individuals as the shareholders. In the case of Skywalk Restaurant Ltd., the board of directors is going to be comprised only of Mr. Cooke because he wants to have sole control of the operation of the business.

It is possible to incorporate a company with one director or any other number of directors that the incorporators choose. In this clause, it is simply necessary to indicate either the number of directors or the minimum and maximum number of directors that you want. Because Mr. Cooke hopes his company will grow, he has said that the minimum number of directors shall be one and the maximum number of directors shall be three.

Clause 5 — Restrictions, if any, on business a corporation may carry on

Unlike the old Companies Act, companies incorporated under the Business Corporations Act have all the powers and rights of a natural person. Accordingly, it is not necessary to go through the rather foolish exercise of listing all of the various objects under which your company can carry on business.

I recommend that unless there are very strong reasons for the company to restrict its business, no restrictions be placed on the type of business that it may carry on.

For tax purposes, it may be necessary to restrict the type of business simply to the holding of assets in order that any gain on the subsequent sale of those assets be deemed as a capital gain and not as income. However, this is a decision you should clear with your accountant.

Clause 6 — Other provisions, if any

Now comes a very important part of the incorporation procedure. The Articles of Incorporation are similar to the structural foundation of a house in that once established, they are very difficult to change. In fact, alterations to the Articles of Incorporation, which are discussed in chapter 5, can only be made by way of a special resolution which requires a two-thirds majority or such greater majority as the Articles of Incorporation require.

The significance of the above is that there are certain provisions that you may wish to include in the Articles because they are necessary to help run the organization and are important enough to act as the structural beams of your company.

For example, the number of people necessary to form a quorum, the majority requirements, the length of notice for a meeting, the location of meetings, and so on may be important provisions for you to add.

Under the Business Corporations Act, these types of provisions can be included in one of three places. They may be inserted into clause 6 of the Articles of Incorporation or they may be part of the by-laws, which are an internal document of the corporation. The by-laws are not part of the public record and they can be amended by the directors at any directors' meeting subject to ratification by a simple majority of the shareholders at the next annual meeting (see chapter 4).

To complicate things even further, the Business Corporations Act states that some of these provisions must be included in the by-laws and some must be included in the Articles; it gives the company discretion on where to put other provisions. Finally, be aware that most or all of these provisions can also be included in a unanimous shareholders' agreement, which will be discussed later.

The by-laws are discussed in chapter 4; however, for purposes of completing the Articles of Incorporation it is also necessary to look at what should be included in the by-laws and what shouldn't.

The basic decision should be based on whether or not you want to entrench certain things in the Articles of Incorporation; once included in the Articles, those provisions will be much more difficult to change than if they are in the by-laws. Accordingly, in our example, Mr. Cooke includes very few additional provisions in the Articles of Incorporation:

(a) Telephone meetings: The Business Corporations Act allows meetings of the directors or shareholders to be held by telephone. Because this is a handy provision, it should be included in the Articles.

(b) Written resolutions: This allows business to be conducted by way of unanimous written resolutions, which will speed up and simplify matters.

(c) Borrowing authority: Mr. Cooke has included a clause giving the directors full authority to borrow funds for and on behalf of the company and to pledge, hypothecate, or mortgage assets of the company in order to raise money; this right is given to the directors in the Business Corporations Act, but financial institutions seem to like to see it in black and white, especially in the incorporating documents of the company. If Mr. Cooke ever needs to get financing very quickly, having this provision in the Articles of Incorporation may help.

There are a number of other provisions that you may or may not wish to include in the Articles of Incorporation. Most are not necessary unless you have specific need for them. Schedule B (see Sample #8) will be all that you need. For purposes of your company, here is a short list of other things that the Articles may include:

(a) Articles may regulate the power of directors to determine to whom, when, and at what price shares may be issued.

(b) Articles may regulate or prohibit share buy-backs by the corporation or redemption or purchase of its redeemable shares.

(c) Articles may provide for a lien on issued shares for debt owing by a shareholder or for a method of enforcement of that lien.

(d) Articles may regulate the powers of directors to make, amend, and repeal by-laws.

(e) Articles may require share qualification for directors.

(f) Articles may confirm that directors' resolutions may be effectively signed by way of fax transmission in addition to having only live signatures.

(g) Articles may require that notices of directors' meetings specify the business or purpose of the meeting.

(h) Articles may require directors' resolutions to be in writing.

(i) Articles may regulate the power of directors to fix remuneration of directors, officers, and employees.

(j) Articles may stipulate other than one vote per share for shareholders and require voting to be other than by show of hands or ballot if demanded.

(k) Articles may require the directors to provide extra financial information at the annual general meeting.

(l) Articles may provide for an audit committee.

Clause 7 — Incorporators

The Business Corporations Act now allows companies to be incorporated with only one shareholder. Accordingly, only Mr. Cooke has signed the Articles. He has given his full name and address (including postal code) and signed his name in clause 7.

If an incorporator is a body corporate, the name is the name of the body corporate and the address that of its registered office. The address of the registered office must be inserted here.

c. OTHER NOTICES REQUIRED TO BE FILED

In addition to Articles of Incorporation and the NUANS report, it is necessary to file two other forms. They are a Notice of Address (Form 3) and a Notice of Directors (Form 6).

Sample #9 shows Mr. Cooke's Notice of Address and Sample #10 his Notice of Directors.

The Business Corporations Act distinguishes between a registered office and a records office for a company. The registered office (see item 3 of the Notice of Address) is the location in the province of Alberta where all legal documents can be served personally or by mail.

A corporation may have a different address for personal service from that of its address for service by mail. The address for personal service of documents of a corporation must be accessible to the public. Mr. Cooke has included his home address as the registered office of the company. Alternatives include your lawyer's or your accountant's office, but check with them prior to listing their addresses because they may have a yearly fee for acting as registered office for your company.

Your registered office will receive a lot of mail from various agencies, including government departments, such as Revenue Canada, Workers' Compensation, etc.; make sure that your registered office is instructed to forward this mail to you.

The records office is the office where all of the important documents of the company, such as the Articles, by-laws, minutes, copies of notices, minute book, etc., must be kept. The records office does not necessarily have to be the same as the registered office but

must be an office accessible to the public during business hours.

If someone commences legal action against your corporation, he or she only needs to serve the registered office for the legal action to proceed. Therefore, make sure your registered office is capable of dealing with this situation should it arise.

Although the registered office must be in Alberta, the records address can be outside the province of Alberta as long as copies of the important documents are kept at an address in Alberta.

The reason for the existence of the records office is to provide a location where certain individuals have access to certain incorporation documents. As already indicated, the Articles of Incorporation is a public document, and any person can search at the Corporate Registry and get a copy of the Articles of Incorporation. However, much of the other information kept at the records office is confidential, and only certain people have access to it.

A shareholder has basically unlimited access to most of the documents kept at the records address. Creditors are also entitled to examine by-laws and amendments, Notices of Directors, etc. Any member of the public can examine the copies of the Notices of Directors and the mortgage registers (see chapter 5 for more on mortgage registers). Under the Business Corporations Act, the use of a postal box number for a registered or records office is not allowed.

Item 2 of the Notice of Address refers to the corporate access number. This is the number issued when the company is incorporated. Obviously, because the company is not yet incorporated, a corporate access number has not been granted, so that item must be left blank.

Mr. Cooke has decided that the best place to keep the records office would be at the restaurant address where he will be carrying on his business.

The Notice of Directors provides information about the directors of the company. For new incorporations, only items 1, 5, 6, and 7 need be completed. Full names and addresses of the directors are required. Ensure that at least one-half of them are Canadian residents. Accordingly, if the company has only one director, that director obviously must be a resident of Canada.

The incorporator of the company need not be the first director, although this is commonly how it is done. In the case of Mr. Cooke's company, since he is going to be the only director, his name and address are put in the appropriate places on the form.

All completed documents should be filled out in duplicate and submitted, along with the filing fee of $300 and a covering form entitled Request for Corporate Services (see Sample #25 later in this book), to:

Corporate Registry
Alberta Consumer and Corporate Affairs
8th Floor, John E. Brownlee Bldg.
10365 — 97 Street
Edmonton, AB T5J 3W7

Note that this office is commonly referred to as the Companies Branch, rather than the Corporate Registry.

The documents normally take between ten days and two weeks to be processed. If they are all in order, the Certificate of Incorporation will be issued immediately. If there are deficiencies in the documents, a deficiency notice will be sent to you indicating the exact reasons for rejection of the forms. Once the documents have been corrected, they may be resubmitted without any additional fee and the processing will continue.

Your effective date of incorporation will be the day that the Companies Branch receives your completed package in satisfactory form. In other words, if you get the paperwork in on August 1, 1997, no matter what date it is subsequently processed, your company's date of incorporation will be August 1, 1997.

d. CERTIFICATE OF INCORPORATION

The Certificate of Incorporation acts almost as a birth certificate: it is formal evidence of the creation of the company. In fact, the date on the Certificate of Incorporation is deemed in law to be conclusive proof of the date that the corporation came into existence.

Sample #11 shows Mr. Cooke's Certificate of Incorporation. The corporation number in the top right-hand corner is the corporate access number; it must be used for all corporate income tax filings, annual summary filings, and other filings with the Companies Branch.

e. PROFESSIONAL CORPORATIONS

Prior to the changes under the Business Corporations Act, professional corporations were the only corporations that were allowed to operate with only one shareholder. This has now, of course, been changed, but professional corporations continue in existence and basically apply to certain professionals, namely architects, certified general accountants, certified management accountants, chartered accountants, chiropractors, dentists, lawyers, and medical doctors.

The words "Professional Corporation" must be the last words in the name of every corporation incorporated as a professional corporation. Most important, the incorporator must send to the Corporate Registry evidence satisfactory to the Registrar of the approval of the Articles of Incorporation by the appropriate professional society. The relevant professional institute must provide *in writing* its approval for the incorporation of its member as a professional corporation.

Articles of Incorporation or Continuance will have to be filed and under clause 6, certain disclaimers about professional liability will have to be included. Professional associations provide the wording for these disclaimers. Those exclusions basically state that the liability of the shareholder is limited except where a company is providing professional services for the group under which it is incorporated (e.g., legal services). In that case, the liability of the shareholders is unlimited; for example, lawyers carrying on business under a professional corporation cannot limit their liability if they are negligent in handling a particular matter. They will have the same liability as they would if they had not incorporated.

Except for legal professional corporations, all shareholders of a professional corporation must be professionals; therefore, there is no way that income splitting can be done between spouses unless both husband and wife are professionals in the same field. Until recently, it was possible to issue shares in a lawyer's professional corporation to non-lawyers. This right has now been revoked.

The debate continues to rage as to whether or not there are tax advantages in forming a professional corporation. There are certain benefits available, such as the small business deduction, tax deferrals, housing loans, benefit plans, and estate planning. If family members can hold shares, this will allow income splitting (see chapter 8). On the negative side, there is an association of corporations tax problem and the possibility of double taxation.

It should be noted, however, that there is no longer any question as to the legitimacy of professional corporations in the eyes of the tax department. Just be sure that all your documents are properly prepared and filed. This includes employment agreements, rollover documents, etc. For a thorough review of the advantages and disadvantages in this area, you should seek proper advice from a tax and corporate law specialist.

SAMPLE #9
NOTICE OF ADDRESS OR
NOTICE OF CHANGE OF ADDRESS

IMPORTANT: PLEASE READ INSTRUCTIONS ON THE BACK OF THIS FORM

BUSINESS CORPORATIONS ACT
(SECTION 19)

FORM 3

Alberta
CONSUMER AND
CORPORATE AFFAIRS

NOTICE OF ADDRESS OR
NOTICE OF CHANGE OF ADDRESS

1. NAME OF CORPORATION:

SKYWALK RESTAURANT LTD.

2. CORPORATE ACCESS NUMBER:

3. ADDRESS OF REGISTERED OFFICE (ONLY A STREET ADDRESS, INCLUDING POSTAL CODE, OR LEGAL LAND DESCRIPTION).

112 Eat Hardy Drive S.W., Calgary, Alberta Z1P 0G0

4. RECORDS ADDRESS (ONLY A STREET ADDRESS, INCLUDING POSTAL CODE, OR LEGAL LAND DESCRIPTION)

c/o SKYWALK RESTAURANT
1504 "Highrise Commercial Centre"
600 - 6th Avenue S.W.
Calgary, Alberta Z1P 0G0

5. ADDRESS FOR SERVICE BY MAIL, IF DIFFERENT FROM ITEM 3 (ONLY A POST OFFICE BOX, INCLUDING POSTAL CODE).

N/A

6. DATE	SIGNATURE	TITLE
April 16, 199-	*Stew Coolee*	President
		TELEPHONE NO.
		297-1234
FOR DEPARTMENTAL USE ONLY		FILED

42

SAMPLE #10
NOTICE OF DIRECTORS OR
NOTICE OF CHANGE OF DIRECTORS

IMPORTANT: PLEASE READ INSTRUCTIONS ON THE BACK OF THIS FORM

BUSINESS CORPORATIONS ACT
(SECTIONS 101, 108 AND 276)

FORM 6

Alberta

CONSUMER AND
CORPORATE AFFAIRS

NOTICE OF DIRECTORS OR
NOTICE OF CHANGE OF DIRECTORS

1. NAME OF CORPORATION:

SKYWALK RESTAURANT

2. ALBERTA CORPORATE ACCESS NUMBER:

3. ON THE _____ DAY OF _____ ,19 _____ , THE FOLLOWING PERSON(S) WERE APPOINTED DIRECTOR(S):

N/A

NAME	MAILING ADDRESS (INCLUDING POSTAL CODE)	RESIDENT CANADIAN?
		YES ☐ NO ☐
		YES ☐ NO ☐
		YES ☐ NO ☐

4. ON THE _____ DAY OF _____ , 19 _____ , THE FOLLOWING PERSON(S) CEASED TO HOLD OFFICE AS DIRECTOR(S):

NAME	MAILING ADDRESS (INCLUDING POSTAL CODE)

5. AS OF THIS DATE, THE DIRECTOR(S) OF THE CORPORATION ARE:

NAME	MAILING ADDRESS (INCLUDING POSTAL CODE)	RESIDENT CANADIAN?
Stew Cooke	112 Eat Hardy Drive S.W. Calgary, Alberta Z1P 0G0	YES ☒ NO ☐
		YES ☐ NO ☐
		YES ☐ NO ☐
		YES ☐ NO ☐

6. TO BE COMPLETED ONLY BY ALBERTA CORPORATIONS:

ARE AT LEAST HALF OF THE MEMBERS OF THE BOARD OF DIRECTORS RESIDENT CANADIANS ?

YES ☒   NO ☐

7. DATE:	SIGNATURE	TITLE
9- 04 18 YEAR MONTH DAY	*Stew Cooke*	President
FOR DEPARTMENTAL USE ONLY		TELEPHONE NUMBER 297-1234
		FILED

CCA-06 106

43

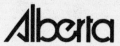

12**345**678
Corporate Access No.

BUSINESS CORPORATIONS ACT

Form 2

CERTIFICATE OF INCORPORATION

- SKYWALK RESTAURANT LTD. -
Name of Corporation

I HEREBY CERTIFY THAT THE ABOVE-MENTIONED CORPORATION, THE ARTICLES OF

INCORPORATION OF WHICH ARE ATTACHED, WAS INCORPORATED UNDER THE

BUSINESS CORPORATIONS ACT OF THE PROVINCE OF ALBERTA.

Registrar of Corporations

April 17, 199-

Date of Incorporation

4
ORGANIZING YOUR COMPANY

In actual fact, most small businesses are nothing more than incorporated partnerships or sole proprietorships. One of the nice things about incorporating is that, with a few exceptions, you can continue your business in exactly the same way that you were carrying on before incorporation while still enjoying the many benefits of incorporation.

However, in order to ensure that you remain entitled to those benefits, it is absolutely necessary that the proper formalities are followed. This means that a minute book must be maintained and proper minutes must be kept of the directors' meetings and shareholders' meetings. Luckily, as you will soon see, a lot of the formalities involved in the actual minute-taking can be eliminated because notice provisions and resolutions can be just as enforceable without notice when signed by all of the directors or shareholders in writing as if formal notice had been given. As well, telephone meetings of directors or shareholders are now allowed.

However, for both tax and legal purposes I recommend that some record be kept of all actions taken in a company involving elections, resignations of directors, share issuances, and transfers, etc. The worst thing that you can possibly do is back date documents in order to attempt to provide back-up evidence for something. This borders dangerously close on fraud or, if tax related, tax evasion, and is certainly not advised.

Once the company is set up and functioning, it will require only a modest amount of time on a yearly basis to ensure

that these matters are properly documented; the time is well spent.

a. MINUTE BOOK

By now, you have received your Certificate of Incorporation and filed copies of the Notice of Address, Notice of Directors, and Articles of Incorporation.

Just like the birth of a child, however, things do not end with the delivery of a newborn. There is a lot of work to be done in raising the new arrival in such a way that it will grow, prosper, and, sooner or later, begin to run itself.

The first requirement is for you to buy some form of binder or minute book that will allow you to properly organize all of the documents that have been prepared and that you will be preparing from time to time.

Minute books with all the necessary dividers are available in various stores or from the publisher. You may make your own using a three-ring binder and some dividers. I suggest that your minute book be divided into sections with the following headings on the dividers:

(a) Certificate of Incorporation

(b) Articles of Incorporation and Amendments

(c) Notices Filed with the Registrar of Companies

(d) Directors' Minutes

(e) Shareholders' Minutes

(f) Directors' Register

(g) Securities' Register

(h) Shareholders' Ledger

(i) Mortgage Register

(j) Share Certificates

(k) Unanimous Shareholders' Agreement

(l) Annual Corporate Filings

(m)Financial Statements and Corporate Tax Returns

(n) By-laws and Amendments

(o) Extra-Provincial Registrations

(p) GST Registrations

(q) Miscellaneous

Keeping all the important corporate information in one place will certainly make the organization and management of the company much easier. As discussed above, certain documents must be maintained at the records office for the company; accordingly, a copy of the corporate minute book should be updated from time to time and maintained at the corporate records office.

b. ORGANIZATIONAL MEETING OF INCORPORATORS

There is an obligation on the first directors of the company to convene an organizational meeting of the company after receiving the Certificate of Incorporation. The directors named in the Notice of Directors (Form 6) are deemed to be the first directors of the company until the first meeting of shareholders. At the first meeting of shareholders, the shareholders can confirm the appointment of those directors or replace them with new directors. It is customary, however, for the first meeting to be a meeting of subscribers or incorporators and the second meeting to be a meeting of shareholders.

Under the Business Corporations Act, five days' notice is required for the initial organizational meeting (unless otherwise changed in the Articles of Incorporation), although a director may waive this notice.

In fact, it may not even be necessary to have a meeting as the minutes are normally just a recitation of standard procedures that are required to be recorded. As long as there is no dissension among the directors, this practice will be satisfactory if all of the documents are read thoroughly and signed by the directors.

Now you need to know the items that must be reviewed at this organizational meeting.

1. Election of officers

As discussed in chapter 2, the directors are given the responsibility of electing or appointing officers.

The most important duty that an officer has to do at this point is to act as the signing authority on behalf of the company.

In normal cases, the corporation will appoint both a president and secretary. In Skywalk Restaurant Ltd., Mr. Cooke is appointed president and his wife, Carmel Cooke, is appointed secretary. Their rights and duties are stated in the by-laws.

2. The by-laws

The by-laws of a company are very similar to the "Articles of Association" of a company under the old system. They represent the rules and regulations under which your company is governed and set out the many items that are used by the company in its day-to-day operation.

Unlike the old Articles of Association, the by-laws are internal only and do not have to be filed with the Companies Branch. Only shareholders, directors, officers, and, occasionally, creditors can review them, and they can be changed by the directors from time to time as long as the shareholders ratify those changes.

The clauses that can be included in the by-laws can go on and on; there is no advantage to reviewing them on an item-by-item basis. Sample #12 shows the by-laws adopted by Skywalk Restaurant Ltd. These are basically a standard set of by-laws which can be used by most small non-distributing companies. Pre-printed by-laws are available from the publisher. Note that a company does not need by-laws in order to carry on business, but the adoption of some simple rules is recommended.

3. Share issuances and share certificates

The next portion of the directors' meeting is taken up with issuing shares to the share subscribers. Normally the incorporators are the first subscribers for shares. In our example, Mr. Cooke is in effect the first shareholder of the company. As discussed above, it would be quite in order if no further shares of the company were issued because under the Business Corporations Act, a one-shareholder company is allowed, and there is no requirement that Mr. Cooke have any more than one share.

However, Mr. Cooke wants to issue some more Class A shares to himself, some Class B shares to his wife, and Class E shares to his investor, E. T. Hardy. Accordingly, the minutes state that Mr. Cooke was issued an additional 99 shares to bring his total Class A shareholdings up to 100 shares, Mrs. Cooke was issued 100 Class B shares (which we have already defined as being non-voting shares), and Mr. Hardy was issued 50 Class E shares (which we have already defined as non-voting preferred shares).

The minutes state how much each party paid for his or her shares and the value of each class of share. In this case, Class A and B shares are $1 per share and Class E shares are $50 per share. In other words, Mr. Hardy put $2 500 worth of share capital into the company as an investment, whereas Mr. Cooke and his wife only put in $100 each. However, the Cookes' contribution will be the expertise and day-to-day labor they intend to put into the business rather than cash.

The minutes then go on to approve the form of share certificates to be used. There is a different certificate for each of the Class A, B, and E shares, and they are numbered consecutively within each class, i.e., A-1, A-2, A-3, B-1, B-2, B-3, in order to distinguish different shareholder certificates within each class of shares.

Each share certificate must have on it the rights, liabilities, and restrictions on the transfer of the share certificate. (See Samples #13, #14, and #15.)

The share certificates should also be stamped with the words "non-negotiable," giving notice to the world that, unlike dollar bills, these shares cannot be freely transferred from one party to another.

In preparing the share certificates, you should also make the necessary notations in the corporate minute book under the headings of Securities Register and Shareholders' Ledger. Sample #16 of the Securities Register and Sample #17 of the Shareholder's Ledger for Skywalk Restaurant Ltd. will give you an idea of how they can be set up.

The share certificates themselves are probably safest if attached to the minute book and kept there. Share certificates can be purchased at stationery stores or from the publisher, but it is still difficult to replace share certificates that have been issued to shareholders and are subsequently misplaced.

Chapter 5 discusses how shares can be transferred from one party to another.

4. Auditors

An auditor performs an important and useful function on behalf of a company and can be a source of great protection for shareholders.

The appointment of an auditor is within the control of the shareholders, who are authorized to appoint an auditor at each annual meeting. The directors, however, can appoint an auditor to hold office until the first annual meeting; they are also required to fill vacancies.

BY-LAW NO. 1

A by-law relating generally to the conduct of the affairs of

BE IT ENACTED AND IT IS HEREBY ENACTED as a by-law of

(hereinafter called the "Corporation") as follows:

Division One
INTERPRETATION

1.01 In this by-law and all other by-laws of the Corporation, unless the context otherwise specifies or requires:

"Act" means the Business Corporations Act of Alberta, as from time to time amended and every statute that may be substituted therefor and, in the case of such substitution, any references in the by-laws of the Corporation to provisions of the Act shall be read as references to the substituted provisions thereof in the new statute or statutes;

"Appoint" includes "elect" and vice versa;

"Articles" means the Articles of Incorporation of the Corporation filed _____ as from time to time amended supplemented or restated;

"Board" means the board of directors of the Corporation;

"By-laws" means this by-law and all other by-laws of the Corporation from time to time in force and effect;

"Cheque" includes a draft;

"Meeting of Shareholders" includes an annual or other general meeting of shareholders and a special meeting of shareholders; "special meeting of shareholders" includes a meeting of any class or classes of shareholders;

"Recorded Address" means in the case of a shareholder his address as recorded in the securities register; and in the case of joint shareholders the address appearing in the securities register in respect of such joint holding or the first address so appearing if there is more than one; and in the case of a director, officer, auditor or member of a committee of the board, his latest address as recorded in the records of the Corporation;

"Regulations" means the regulations under the Act as published or from time to time amended and every regulation that may be substituted therefor and, in the case of such substitution, any references in the by-laws of the Corporation to provisions of the Regulations shall be read as references to the substituted provisions therefor in the new regulations;

"Resident Albertan" means an individual who is ordinarily resident in Alberta or, if not ordinarily resident in Alberta, is a member of a class of persons prescribed by Regulations and, in any case,

(a) is a Canadian citizen, or

(b) has been lawfully admitted to Canada for permanent residence;

"Signing Officer" means, in relation to any instrument, any person authorized to sign the same on behalf of the corporation by virtue of Section 3.01 of this by-law or by a resolution passed pursuant thereto;

SELF-COUNSEL PRESS
1481 Charlotte Road
North Vancouver, British Columbia V7J 1H1
FORM CDN-INC-ALT (4-1) 88

1

"Unanimous Shareholder Agreement" means an otherwise lawful written agreement among all shareholders of the corporation, or among all such shareholders and a person who is not a shareholder, that restricts, in whole or in part, the powers of the directors to manage the business and affairs of the Corporation as from time to time amended.

Save as aforesaid, all terms which are contained in the by-laws of the Corporation and which are defined in the Act or the Regulations shall have the meanings given to such terms in the Act or the Regulations. Words importing the singular number include the plural and vice versa; the masculine shall include the feminine; and the word "person" shall include an individual, partnership, association, body corporate, corporation, company, syndicate, trustee, executor, administrator, legal representative, and any number or aggregate of persons.

Division Two

BORROWING, BANKING AND SECURITIES

2.01 Borrowing Power: Without limiting the borrowing powers of the Corporation as set forth in the Act, but subject to the articles and any unanimous shareholder agreement, the board may from time to time on behalf of the Corporation, without authorization of the shareholders:

    (a)   borrow money upon the credit of the Corporation;

    (b)   issue, reissue, sell or pledge bonds, debentures, note or other evidences of indebtedness or guarantee of the Corporation, whether secured or unsecured;

    (c)   to the extent permitted by the Act, give a guarantee on behalf of the Corporation to secure performance of any present or future indebtedness, liability or obligation of any person; and

    (d)   mortgage, hypothecate, pledge or otherwise create a security interest in all or any currently owned or subsequently acquired real or personal, moveable or immoveable, property of the Corporation including book debts, rights, powers, franchises and undertakings, to secure any such bonds, debentures, note or other evidences of indebtedness or guarantee or any other present or future indebtedness, liability or obligation of the Corporation.

Nothing in this section limits or restricts the borrowing of money by the Corporation on bills of exchange or promissory notes made, drawn, accepted or endorsed by or on behalf of the Corporation.

2.01A(a)   Raise and assist in raising money for, and to add by way of bonus, loan, promise, endorsement, guarantee or otherwise any person or Company whether or not the Company has business relations with that person or Company and to guarantee the performance or fulfillment of any contracts or obligations of any such person or Company, and in particular to guarantee the payment of the principal of and interest on securities, mortgages and liabilities of any such person or Company;

    (b)   The Directors may delegate the powers contained in this Article such Officers or Directors of the Corporation and to such extent and in such manner as may be set out in the by-laws;

    (c)   Lend to or guarantee, with or without security, the contracts of any person or Company, wheresoever incorporated, having dealings or business relations with the Corporation or with whom the Corporation proposes to have dealings or business relations, the contracts of any person or company proposing to buy or owning shares of the capital stock of the Corporation securing or evidencing an obligation in respect of the purchase price thereof or facilitating or evidencing any borrowing by such person or Company in respect of the purchase price of such shares, or otherwise.

2.02 Delegation: The board may from time to time delegate to a committee of the board, a director or an officer of the Corporation or any other person as may be designated by the board all or any of the powers conferred on the board by the preceding section of this by-law or by the Act to such extent and in such manner as the board may determine at the time of such delegation.

2.03 Banking Arrangements: The banking business of the Corporation including, without limitation, the borrowing of money and the giving of security therefore, shall be transacted with such banks, trust companies or other bodies corporate or organizations as may from time to time be designated by or under the authority of the board. Such banking business or any part thereof shall be transacted under such agreements, instructions and delegations of powers as the board may from time to time prescribe.

2.04 Custody of Securities: All shares and securities owned by the Corporation shall be lodged (in the name of the Corporation) with a chartered bank or a trust company or in a safety deposit box or, if so authorized by resolution of the board of directors, with such other depositaries or in such other manner as may be determined from time to time by the board of directors.

2

All share certificates, bonds, debentures, notes or other obligations belonging to the Corporation may be held in the name of a nominee or nominees of the Corporation (and if held in the names of more than one nominee shall be held in the names of the nominees jointly with the right of survivorship) and shall be endorsed in blank with endorsement guaranteed in order to enable transfer to be completed and registration to be effected.

2.05 Voting Shares and Securities in Other Corporations: All of the shares or other securities carrying voting rights of any other body corporate held from time to time by the Corporation, other than shares it beneficially owns in its holding body corporate, may be voted at any and all meetings of shareholders, bondholders, debenture holder or holders of other securities (as the case may be) of such body corporate and in such manner and by such person or persons as the board of directors of the Corporation shall from time to time determine. The proper signing officers of the Corporation may also execute and deliver for and on behalf of the Corporation proxies and/or arrange for the issuance of voting certificates and/or other evidence of the right to vote in such names as they may determine without the necessity of a resolution or other action by the board of directors.

Division Three

EXECUTION OF INSTRUMENTS

3.01 Deeds, transfers, assignments, contracts, obligations, certificates and other instruments may be signed on behalf of the Corporation by two persons, one of whom holds the office of chairman of the board, managing director, president, vice-president or director and the other of whom holds one of the said offices or the office of secretary, treasurer, assistant secretary or assistant treasurer or any other office created by by-law or by the board. In addition, the board or the said two persons may from time to time direct the manner in which and the person or persons by whom any particular instrument or class of instruments may or shall be signed. Any signing officer may affix the corporate seal to any instrument requiring the same, but no instrument is invalid merely because the corporate seal is not affixed thereto.

3.02 Cheques, Drafts and Notes: All cheques, drafts or orders for the payment of money and all notes and acceptances and bills of exchange shall be signed by such officer or officers or person or persons, whether or not officers of the Corporation, and in such manner as the board of directors may from time to time designate by resolution.

Division Four

DIRECTORS

4.01 Number: The board of directors shall consist of the number fixed by the articles, or where the articles specify a variable number, the number of directors shall be a minimum of one (1) and a maximum of _____ , at least half of whom shall be resident Canadians.

4.02 Election and Term: Subject to the articles or a unanimous shareholder agreement the election of directors shall take place at each annual meeting of shareholders and all the directors then in office, unless elected for a longer period of time, shall retire but, if qualified, shall be eligible for re-election. The number of directors to be elected at any such meeting shall, subject to the articles or a unanimous shareholder agreement, be the number of directors then in office, or the number of directors whose terms of office expire at the meeting, as the case may be, except that if cumulative voting is not required by the articles and the articles otherwise permit, the shareholders may resolve to elect some other number of directors. Where the shareholders adopt an amendment to the articles to increase the number or minimum number of directors, the shareholders may, at the meeting at which they adopt the amendment, elect the additional number of directors authorized by the amendment. If an election of directors is not held at the proper time, the incumbent directors shall continue in office until their successors are elected. If the articles provide for cumulative voting each director elected by shareholders (but not directors elected or appointed by creditors or employees) ceases to hold office at the annual meeting and every shareholder entitled to vote at an election of directors has the right to cast votes for the directors to be elected equal to the number of votes attached to the shares held by him multiplied by the number of directors he is entitled to vote for, and he may cast all such votes in favor of one candidate or distribute them among the candidates in such manner as he sees fit. If he has voted for more than one candidate without specifying the distribution among such candidates he shall be deemed to have divided his votes equally among the candidates for whom he voted.

4.03 Removal of Directors: Subject to the Act, the shareholders may by ordinary resolution passed at a meeting specially called for such purpose remove any director from office, except a director elected by employees or creditors pursuant to the articles or a unanimous shareholder agreement, and the vacancy created by such removal may be filled at the same meeting, failing which it may be filled by the board. Provided, however, that if the articles provide for cumulative voting no director shall be removed pursuant to this section where the votes cast against the resolution for his removal would, if cumulatively voted at an election of the full board, be sufficient to elect one or more directors.

3

50

4.04 Qualification: No person shall be qualified for election as a director if he is less than 18 years of age; if he is of unsound mind and has been so found by a Court in Canada or elsewhere, if he is not an individual; or if he has the status of a bankrupt. A director need not be a shareholder.

4.05 Consent: No election or appointment of a person as director shall be effective unless:

(a) he was present at the meeting when he was elected or appointed and did not refuse to act as a director, or

(b) he consents in writing to act as a director before his election or appointment or within ten days thereafter, or

(c) he acts as a director pursuant to the election or appointment.

4.06 Vacation of Office: A director ceases to hold office when he dies; he is removed from office by the shareholders or by creditors or employees who elected him, as the case may be; he ceases to be qualified for election as a director; he be convicted of an indictable offence; or his written resignation is sent or delivered to the Corporation, or, if a time is specified in such resignation, at the time so specified, whichever is later.

4.07 Committee of Directors: The directors may appoint from among their number one or more committees of directors, however designated, and subject to Section 110 of the Act may delegate to any such committee any of the powers of the directors. At least half of the members of any such committee shall be resident Canadians.

4.08 Transaction of Business: Subject to the provisions of Section 5.09 the powers of a committee of directors may be exercised by a meeting at which a quorum is present or by resolution in writing signed by all the members of such committee who would have been entitled to vote on that resolution at a meeting of the committee. Meetings of such committee may be held at any place in or outside Canada.

4.09 Advisory Bodies: The board may from time to time appoint such advisory bodies as it may deem advisable, but the functions of any such other committees shall be advisory only.

4.10 Procedure: Unless otherwise determined by the board, each committee and advisory body shall have the power to fix its quorum at not less than a majority of its members, to elect its chairman and to regulate its procedure.

4.11 Remuneration and Expenses: Subject to any unanimous shareholder agreement, the directors shall be paid such remuneration for their services as the board may from time to time determine. The directors shall also be entitled to be reimbursed for travelling and other expenses properly incurred by them in attending meetings of the board or any committee thereof. Nothing herein contained shall preclude any director from serving the Corporation in any other capacity and receiving remuneration therefor.

4.12 Subscribers first directors: The subscribers hereto shall be the first directors of the Corporation, unless the Corporation has been incorporated and directors elected prior to the adoption of these articles.

4.13 Alternate directors: Any director may, at any time and from time to time, appoint any other person to be his alternate to act in his place at any meeting of directors at which he is not personally present, and may at any time remove any alternate director appointed by him and appoint another in his place. The notice of appointment may name more than one person in order of preference to act as alternate, if the other persons named in priority are not present at any meeting. An alternate director shall not be entitled to receive any notice of meetings of directors or any remuneration from the Corporation, but he shall otherwise have the powers and be subject in all respects to the terms and conditions existing with reference to the other directors of the Corporation. Any appointment so made may be revoked at any time by the appointor. An alternate director shall, ipso facto, cease to be an alternate director if his appointor ceases for any reason to be a director. Every person acting as an alternate director shall alone be responsible to the Corporation for his own acts and defaults, and he shall not be deemed to be the agent of or for the director appointing him. The director so appointing shall not be responsible for the acts and defaults of an alternate director so appointed. All appointments and removals of alternate directors made by any director in pursuance of this by-law shall be in writing under the name of the director making the same, and shall be sent to or left at the registered office or the head office of the Corporation or sent to or delivered to the Secretary of the Corporation. Any appointment of an alternate director may be either for a specific meeting or for all meetings during a specific period of time.

4

SAMPLE #12 — Continued

Division Five

MEETING OF DIRECTORS

5.01 Place of Meeting: Meetings of the board of directors and of committees of directors (if any) may be held within or outside Alberta.

5.02 Notice of Meeting: Notice of the time and place of each meeting of the board shall be given in the manner provided in Section 13.01 to each director not less than 48 hours before the time when the meeting is to be held. A notice of a meeting of directors need not specify the purpose of or the business to be transacted at the meeting except where the Act requires such purpose or business to be specified, including, if required by the Act, any proposal to:

(a) submit to the shareholders any question or matter requiring approval of the shareholders;

(b) fill a vacancy among the directors or in the office of auditor;

(c) issue securities;

(d) declare dividends;

(e) purchase, redeem or otherwise acquire shares issued by the Corporation;

(f) pay a commission for the sale of shares;

(g) approve a management proxy circular;

(h) approve a take-over bid circular or directors' circular;

(i) approve any annual financial statements; or

(j) adopt, amend or repeal by-laws.

Provided, however, that a director may in any manner waive notice of a meeting and attendance of a director at a meeting of directors shall constitute a waiver of notice of the meeting except where a director attends a meeting for the express purpose of objecting to the transaction of any business on the grounds that the meeting is now lawfully called.

For the first meeting of the board of directors to be held immediately following an election of directors or for a meeting of the board of directors at which a director is to be appointed to fill a vacancy in the board, no notice of such meeting shall be necessary to the newly elected or appointed director or directors in order to legally constitute the meeting, provided that a quorum of the directors is present.

5.03 Adjourned Meeting: Notice of an adjourned meeting of the board is not required if the time and place of the adjourned meeting is announced at the original meeting.

5.04 Regular Meetings: The board may appoint a day or days in any month or months for regular meetings of the board at a place and hour to be named. A copy of any resolution of the board fixing the place and time of such regular meetings shall be sent to each director forthwith after being passed, and forthwith to each director subsequently elected or appointed, but no other notice shall be required for any such regular meeting except where the Act or this by-law requires the purpose thereof or the business to be transacted thereat to be specified.

5.05 Chairman and Secretary: The Chairman of any meeting of the board shall be the first mentioned of such of the following officers as have been appointed and who is a director and is present at the meeting: chairman of the board, managing director or president. If no such officer is present, the directors present shall choose one of their number to be chairman. The secretary of the Corporation shall act as secretary at any meeting of the board, and if the secretary of the Corporation be absent, the chairman of the meeting shall appoint a person who need not be a director to act as secretary of the meeting.

5.06 Quorum: Subject to the following section, the quorum for the transaction of business at any meeting of the board shall consist of a majority of the directors holding office or such greater number of directors as the board may from time to time determine.

5.07 Half Canadian Representation at Meetings: The Board shall not transact business at a meeting, other than filling a vacancy in the Board, unless at least half of the directors present are resident Canadians, except where:

(a) a resident Canadian director who is unable to be present approves in writing or by telephone or other telecommunication facilities the business transacted at the meeting; and

(b) at least half of the members present would have been resident Canadians had that director been present at the meeting.

5

5.08 Voting: Questions arising at any meeting of the board of directors shall be decided by a majority of votes. In case of an equality of votes the chairman of the meeting, in addition to his original vote, shall have a second or casting vote.

5.09 Meeting by Telephone: If all the directors of the Corporation consent, a director may participate in a meeting of the board or a committee of the board by means of such telephone or other communication facilities as permit all persons participating in the meeting to hear each other, and a director participating in such a meeting by such means is deemed to be present at the meeting. Any such consent shall be effective whether given before or after the meeting to which it relates and may be given with respect to all meetings of the board and of committees of the board.

5.10 Resolution in Lieu of Meeting: Notwithstanding any of the foregoing provisions of this by-law, a resolution in writing either ordinary or special, signed by all the Directors entitled to vote on that resolution at a meeting of the directors or a committee of directors, if any is as valid as if it had been passed at a meeting of the directors or the committee of directors, if any.

5.11 Minutes: Minutes of any meeting of the board or of any committee of the board, if purporting to be signed by the chairman of such meeting or by the chairman of the next succeeding meeting, shall be receivable as prima facie evidence of the matters stated in such minutes.

5.12 Management and business vested in the board: The management and conduct of the business and affairs of the Corporation shall be vested in the board, which, in addition to the powers and authorities by these by-laws or otherwise expressly conferred upon it, may exercise all such powers and do all such acts and things as may be exercised or done by the Corporation and are not hereby or by statute expressly directed or required to be exercised or done by the members.

Division Six

PROTECTION OF DIRECTORS, OFFICERS AND OTHERS

6.01 Conflict of Interest: A director or officer shall not be disqualified by his office, or be required to vacate his office, by reason only that he is a party to, or is a director or officer or has a material interest in any person who is a party to, a material contract or proposed material contract with the Corporation or a subsidiary thereof. Such a director or officer shall, however, disclose the nature and extent of his interest in the contract at the time and in the manner provided by the Act. Any such contract or proposed contract shall be referred to the board or shareholders for approval even if such contract is one that in the ordinary course of the Corporation's business would not require approval by the board or shareholders. Subject to the provisions of the Act, a director shall not by reason only of his office be accountable to the Corporation or to its shareholders for any profit or gain realized from such a contract or transaction, and such contract or transaction shall not be void or voidable by reason only of the director's interest therein, provided that the required declaration and disclosure of interest is properly made, the contract or transaction is approved by the directors or shareholders, and it is fair and reasonable to the Corporation at the time it was approved and, if required by the Act, the director refrains from voting as a director on the contract or transaction and absents himself from the director's meeting at which the contract is authorized or approved by the directors, except attendance for the purpose of being counted in the quorum.

6.02 Limitation of Liability: Every director and officer of the Corporation in exercising his powers and discharging his duties shall act honestly and with good faith with a view to the best interests of the Corporation and exercise the care, diligence and skill that a reasonably prudent person would exercise in comparable circumstances. Subject to the foregoing, no director or officer for the time being of the Corporation shall be liable for the acts, receipts, neglects or defaults of any other director or officer or employee or for joining in any receipt or act for conformity, or for any loss, damage or expense happening to the Corporation through the insufficiency or deficiency of title to any property acquired by the Corporation or for or on behalf of the Corporation for the insufficiency or deficiency of any security in or upon which any of the moneys of or belonging to the Corporation shall be placed out or invested or for any loss, conversion, misapplication or misappropriation of or any damage resulting from any dealings with any moneys, securities or other assets belonging to the Corporation or for any other loss, damage or misfortune whatever which may happen in the execution of the duties of his respective office or trust or in relation thereto; provided that nothing herein shall relieve any director or officer from the duty to act in accordance with the Act and the regulations thereunder or from liability for any breach thereof. The directors for the time being of the Corporation shall not be under any duty or responsibility in respect of any contract, act or transaction whether or not made, done or entered into the name or on behalf of the Corporation, except such as shall have been submitted to and authorized or approved by the board of directors.

6

6.03 Indemnity: Subject to the Section 119 of the Act, the Corporation shall indemnify a director or officer, a former director or officer, or a person who acts or acted at the Corporation's request as a director or officer of a body corporate of which the Corporation is or was a shareholder or creditor, and his heirs, executors, administrators and other legal representatives, from and against,

(a) any liability and all costs, charges and expenses that he sustains or incurs in respect of any action, suit or proceeding that is proposed or commenced against him for or in respect of anything done or permitted by him in respect of the execution of the duties of his office; and

(b) all other costs, charges and expenses that he sustains or incurs in respect of the affairs of the Corporation;

except where such liability relates to his failure to act honestly and in good faith with a view to the best interests of the Corporation.

The Corporation shall also indemnify such persons in such other circumstances as the Act permits or requires. Nothing in this section shall limit the right of any person entitled to indemnity to claim indemnity apart from the provisions of this section.

6.04 Insurance: Subject to the Act, the Corporation may purchase and maintain insurance for the benefit of any person referred to in the preceding section against any liability incurred by him in his capacity as a director or officer of the Corporation or of any body corporate where he acts or acted in that capacity at the Corporation's request.

6.05 Submission of Contracts or Transactions to Shareholders for Approval: The board of directors in its discretion may submit any contract, act or transaction for approval or ratification at any annual meeting of the shareholders or at any special meeting of the shareholders called for the purpose of considering the same and, subject to the provisions of Section 115 of the Act, any such contract, act or transaction that shall be approved or ratified or confirmed by a resolution passed by a majority of the votes cast at any such meeting (unless any different or additional requirement is imposed by the Act or by the Corporation's articles or any other by-law) shall be as valid and as binding upon the Corporation and upon all the shareholders as though it had been approved, ratified or confirmed by every shareholder of the Corporation.

6.06 Action by the Board: Subject to any unanimous shareholder agreement, the board shall manage the business and affairs of the Corporation. The powers of the board may be exercised at a meeting (subject to Sections 4.08 and 4.09) at which a quorum is present or by resolution in writing signed by all the directors entitled to vote on that resolution at a meeting of the board. Where there is a vacancy in the board, the remaining directors may exercise all the powers of the board so long as a quorum remains in office. Where the Corporation has only one director, that director may constitute a meeting.

6.07 Vacancies: Subject to the Act, a quorum of the board may fill a vacancy in the board, except a vacancy resulting from an increase in the number or minimum number of directors or from a failure of the shareholders to elect the number or minimum number of directors. In the absence of a quorum of the board, or if the vacancy has arisen from a failure of the shareholders to elect the number or minimum number of directors, the board shall forthwith call a special meeting of the shareholders to fill the vacancy. If the board fails to call such meeting or if there are no such directors then in office, any shareholder may call the meeting.

6.08 Calling of Meetings: Meetings of the board shall be held from time to time and at such place as the board, the chairman of the board, the managing director, the president or any two directors may determine.

Division Seven

OFFICERS

7.01 Election or Appointment: Subject to any unanimous shareholder agreement, the board from time to time shall elect or appoint a president or a secretary or both, and may elect or appoint one or more vice-presidents (to which title may be added words indicating seniority or function), a general manager, a treasurer and such other officers as the board may determine, including one or more assistants to any of the officers so elected or appointed. The board from time to time may also elect or appoint a chairman of the board, who must be a director and a resident Albertan, but otherwise the officers of the Corporation need not be resident Albertans or directors of the Corporation. Two or more offices may be held by the same person. The board may specify the duties of and in accordance with this by-law and the law, delegate to such officers powers to manage the business and affairs of the Corporation.

7.02 Chairman of the Board: The chairman of the board shall, when present, preside at all meetings of the board of directors, committees of directors and, in the absence of the president, at all meetings of shareholders. In addition, the board may assign to him any of the powers and duties that may by the provisions of this by-law be assigned to the managing director or to the president; and he shall have such other powers and duties as the board may specify.

7

7.03 Managing Director: The managing director, if any shall be a resident Canadian, and exercise such powers and have such authority as may be delegated to him by the board of directors in accordance with the provisions of Section 110 of the Act and, in particular, the board may delegate to him such of the powers and duties as may be assigned by this by-law to a general manager or manager.

7.04 President:

   (i)   The board, from time to time, may elect from among its number, a President.

   (ii)   The President shall be the chief executive officer of the corporation, and preside at all General Meetings and, in the absence or non-appointment of the Chairman of the Board, shall also preside at meetings of the Board. He shall have general and active management of the business and affairs of the Corporation, and without limitation to the foregoing:

      (1)   he shall have general superintendence and direction of all the other officers of the Corporation;

      (2)   he shall submit the annual report of the board, if any, and the annual balance sheets and financial statements of the business and affairs and reports on the financial position of the Corporation as required by the Statutes to the Annual General Meeting and from time to time he shall report to the board of all matters within his knowledge which the interest of the Corporation requires to be brought to their attention;

      (3)   he shall be ex-officio a member of all standing committees.

7.05 Vice-President: During the absence or disability of the president, his duties shall be performed and his powers exercised by the vice-president or, if there are more than one, by the vice-president designated from time to time by the board for the president; provided, however, that a vice-president who is not a director shall not preside as chairman at any meeting of directors or of a committee of directors. A vice-president shall have such other powers and duties as the board or the president may prescribe.

7.06 Secretary: The secretary or if none is appointed, the President, shall attend and be the secretary of all meetings of the board, shareholders and committees of the board and shall enter or cause to be entered in records kept for that purpose minutes of all proceedings thereat; he shall give or cause to be given, as and when instructed, all notices to shareholders, directors, officers, auditors and members of committees of the board; he shall be the custodian of the stamp or mechanical device generally used for affixing the corporate seal of the Corporation and of all books, papers, records, documents and instruments belonging to the Corporation, except when some other officer or agent has been appointed for that purpose; and he shall have such other powers and duties as the board or the chief executive officer may specify.

7.07 Treasurer: The treasurer shall keep proper accounting records in compliance with the Act and shall be responsible for the deposit of money, the safekeeping of the securities and the disbursement of funds of the Corporation; he shall render to the board whenever required an account of all his transactions and he shall have such other powers and duties as the board or the chief executive officer may specify.

7.08 General Manager or Manager: If elected or appointed, the general manager shall have, subject to the authority of the board, the manager director, if any, and the president, full power to manage and direct the business and affairs of the Corporation (except such matters and duties as by law must be transacted or performed by the board of directors and/or by the shareholders) and to employ and discharge agents and employees of the Corporation or may delegate to him or them any lesser authority. A general manager or manager shall conform to all lawful orders given to him by the board of directors of the Corporation and shall at all reasonable times give to the directors or any of them all information they may require regarding the affairs of the Corporation. Any agent or employee appointed by a general manager or manager shall be subject to discharge by the board of directors.

7.09 Powers and Duties of Other Officers: The powers and duties of all other officers shall be such as the terms of their engagement call for or as the board, the managing director, or the President may specify. Any of the powers and duties of an officer to whom an assistant has been appointed may be exercised and performed by such assistant, unless the board or the chief executive officer otherwise directs.

7.10 Variation of Powers and Duties: The board may from time to time and subject to the provisions of the Act, vary, add to, or limit the powers and duties of any officer.

7.11 Term of Office: The board, in its discretion, may remove any officer of the Corporation, without prejudice to such officer's rights under any employment contract. Otherwise each officer appointed by the board shall hold office until his successor is appointed, or until his earlier resignation.

7.12 Vacancies: If the office of any officer of the Corporation shall be or become vacant by reason of death, resignation, disqualification or otherwise, the directors by resolution shall, in the case of the president or the secretary, and may, in the case of any other office, appoint a person to fill such vacancy.

8

7.13 Remuneration and Removal: The remuneration of all officers appointed by the board of directors shall be determined from time to time by resolution of the board of directors. The fact that any officer or employee is a director or shareholder of the Corporation shall not disqualify him from receiving such remuneration as may be determined. All officers, in the absence of agreement to the contrary, shall be subject to removal by resolution of the board of directors at any time, with or without cause.

7.14 Agents and Attorneys: The Corporation, by or under the authority of the board, shall have power from time to time to appoint agents or attorneys for the Corporation in or outside Canada with such powers (including the power to sub-delegate) of management, administration or otherwise as may be thought fit.

7.15 Conflict of Interest: An officer shall disclose his interest in any material contract or proposed material contract with the Corporation.

7.16 Fidelity Bonds: The board may require such officers, employees and agents of the Corporation as the board deems advisable to furnish bonds for the faithful discharge of their powers and duties, in such forms and with such surety as the board may from time to time determine.

7.17 Executive Committee:

(a)   Whenever the number of directors constituting the board shall consist of more than six (6), the board may appoint not less than three (3) of their number to constitute an Executive Committee, of whom a majority shall constitute a quorum, and who may meet at stated times or on notice to all or any of their own number; the members of such Committee shall advise with and aid the officers and the board in all matters concerning the Corporation's interests and in the management of its business and affairs and generally perform such duties and exercise such powers as may be directed or delegated to such Committee by the board from time to time. The board may delegate to such Committee authority to exercise such of its powers while the board is not in session as the board may designate. Unless and until the board otherwise determines, the president and any directors elected by the board shall constitute the Executive Committee of the Corporation and shall be and are hereby vested with authority to exercise all of the powers of the board while such board is not in session, except such powers as the Statutes are required to be exercised by the board.

(b)   The Executive Committee may act by the written consent of a quorum thereof, although not formally convened.

(c)   The Executive Committee shall keep minutes of its proceedings and report the same to the board at the next meeting thereof.

(d)   A majority of the Executive Committee shall be Canadian residents.

Division Eight

SHAREHOLDERS' MEETINGS

8.01 Annual Meetings: Subject to Section 127 of the Act, the annual meeting of shareholders shall be held at such time and on such day in each year and, subject to Section 8.03, at such place or places as the board, the chairman of the board, the managing director or the president may from time to time determine, for the purpose of considering the financial statements and reports required by the Act to be placed before the annual meeting, elected directors, appointing an auditor if required by the Act or the articles, and for the transaction of such other business as may properly be brought before the meeting.

8.02 Special Meetings: The board, the chairman of the board, the managing director or the president shall have the power to call a special meeting of shareholders at any time. A special meeting may also be called by any shareholder or director on the refusal or inability of the above to call one, provided the caller of the meeting bears all of the expenses of calling and holding the meeting.

8.03 Place of Meetings: Meetings of shareholders shall be held at any place within Alberta as the directors may by resolution determine or, if all the shareholders entitled to vote at the meeting so agree or if the articles so provide, outside Alberta.

8.04 Record Date for Notice: The board may fix in advance a date, preceding the date of any meeting of shareholders by not more than 50 days and not less than 21 days, as a record for the determination of shareholders entitled to notice of the meeting. If no record date is fixed, the record date for the determination of the shareholders entitled to receive notice of the meeting shall be the close of business on the date immediately preceding the day on which the notice is given or, if no notice is given, the day on which the meeting is held.

9

8.05 Notice: A printed, written or typewritten notice stating the day, hour and place of each meeting of shareholders shall be given in the manner provided in Section 13.01 not less than 7 nor more than 30 days before the date of the meeting to each director, to the auditor, and to each shareholder who at the close of business on the record date for notice is entered in the securities register as the holder of one or more shares carrying the right to vote at the meeting. Notice of a meeting of shareholders called for any purpose other than consideration of the financial statements and auditor's report, election of directors and re-appointment of the incumbent auditor shall state the nature of such business in sufficient detail to permit the shareholders to form a reasoned judgment thereon and shall state the text of any special resolution to be submitted to the meeting.

8.06 Right to Vote: At any meeting of shareholders, every person shall be entitled to vote who, on the record date, or if no record date is set, at the close of business on the date preceding the date notice is sent, or if no notice is sent, on the date of the meeting, is entered in the securities register as the holder of one or more shares carrying the right to vote at such meeting, except:

    (a)   that where such person transfers his shares after the record date is set, or if no record date is set, after the close of business on the date preceding the date notice of the meeting is sent to shareholders and

    (b)   the transferee, at least 10 days prior to the meeting, produces properly endorsed share certificates to the secretary or transfer agent of the Corporation or otherwise establishes his ownership of the share

in which case the transferee may vote those shares. If notice is not sent, the transferee may establish his ownership to the shares in the manner aforesaid at any time prior to the holding of the meeting.

8.07 Waiver of Notice: A shareholder and any other person entitled to attend a meeting of shareholders may in any manner waive notice of a meeting of shareholders and attendance of any such person at a meeting of shareholders shall constitute a waiver of notice of the meeting except where such person attends a meeting for the express purpose of objecting to the transaction of any business on the grounds that the meeting is not lawfully called.

8.08 Chairman, Secretary and Scrutineers: The president or, in his absence, the chairman of the board, if such an officer has been elected or appointed and is present, otherwise a vice-president who is a shareholder of the Corporation shall be chairman of any meeting of shareholders. If no such officer is present within 15 minutes from the time fixed for holding the meeting, the persons present and those entitled to vote shall choose one of their number to be chairman. If the secretary of the Corporation is absent, the chairman shall appoint some person, who need not be a shareholder, to act as secretary of the meeting, if desired, one or more scrutineers, who need not be shareholders, may be appointed by a resolution or by the chairman with the consent of the Meeting.

8.09 Persons Entitled to be Present: The only persons entitled to be present at a meeting of shareholders shall be those entitled to vote thereat, the directors and auditors of the Corporation and others who, although not entitled to vote, are entitled or required under any provision of the Act or the articles or by-laws to be present at the meeting. Any other person may be admitted only on the invitation of the chairman of the meeting or with the consent of the meeting.

8.10 Quorum: Subject to the Act, a quorum for the transaction of business at any meeting of shareholders shall be __ __ persons present in person, each being a shareholder entitled to vote thereat or a duly appointed proxyholder or representative for a shareholder so entitled. If a quorum is present at the opening of any meeting of shareholders, the shareholders present or represented may proceed with the business of the meeting notwithstanding that a quorum is not present throughout the meeting. If a quorum is not present at the opening of the meeting of shareholders, the shareholders present or represented may adjourn the meeting to a fixed time and place but may not transact any other business. If a meeting is so adjourned to a fixed time and place, then any members present shall then constitute a quorum.

8.11 Participation in Meeting by Telephone: A shareholder or any other person entitled to attend a meeting of shareholders may participate in the meeting by means of telephone or other telecommunication facilities that permit all persons participating in the meeting to hear each other (if all the shareholders entitled to vote at the meeting consent) and a person participating in such a meeting by those means is deemed to be present at the meeting.

8.12 Proxyholders and Representatives: Votes at meetings of the shareholders may be given either personally or by proxy; or, in the case of a shareholder who is a body corporate or association, by an individual authorized by a resolution of the board of directors or governing body of the body corporate or association to represent it at a meeting of shareholders of the Corporation, upon producing a certified copy of such resolution or otherwise establishing his authority to vote to the satisfaction of the secretary or the chairman.

    A proxy shall be executed by the shareholder or his attorney authorized in writing and is valid only at the meeting in respect to which it is given or any adjournment of that meeting. A person appointed by proxy need not be a shareholder.

10

Subject to the regulations, a proxy may be in the following form:

The undersigned shareholder of _____

hereby appoints _____ of _____ ,

or failing him, _____ as the nominee of the undersigned to attend and act for the

undersigned and on behalf of the undersigned at the _____

meeting of the shareholders of the said Corporation to be held on the _____ day of _____ , 19 ____ and at any

adjournment or adjournments thereof.

DATED this _____ day of _____ , 19 ____ .

_____
Signature of Shareholder

8.13 Time for Deposit of Proxies: The board may specify in a notice calling a meeting of shareholders a time, preceding the time of such meeting by not more than 48 hours exclusive of Saturdays and holidays, before which time proxies to be used at such meeting must be deposited. A proxy shall be acted upon only if, prior to the time so specified, it shall have been deposited with the Corporation or an agent thereof specified in such notice or if, no such time having been specified in such notice, it has been received by the secretary of the Corporation or by the chairman of the meeting or any adjournment thereof prior to the time of voting.

8.14 Validity Following Death or Transfer: A vote given in accordance with the terms of a proxy shall be valid notwithstanding the previous death of the principal or transfer of the share with respect to which the vote is given, provided notice in writing of such death or transfer shall not have been received by the Corporation at least 24 hours before the meeting at the place at which the proxies are to be deposited, nor by the chairman of the meeting at the time of the holding of the meeting.

8.15 Joint Shareholders: If two or more persons hold shares jointly, any one of them present in person or duly represented at a meeting of shareholders may, in the absence of the other or others, vote the shares; but if two or more of those persons are present in person or represented and vote, they shall vote as one the shares jointly held by them. If they cannot or do not agree on the vote of their joint holdings then their vote shall not be taken.

8.16 Votes to Govern: At any meeting of shareholders every question shall, unless otherwise required by the articles or by-laws or by-law, be determined by a majority of the votes cast on the question. In case of an equality of votes either upon a show of hands or upon a ballot, the chairman of the meeting shall be entitled to a second or casting vote.

8.17 Show of Hands: Subject to the Act, any question at a meeting of shareholders shall be decided by a show of hands, unless a ballot thereon is required or demanded as hereinafter provided. Upon a show of hands every person who is present and entitled to vote shall have one vote. Whenever a vote by show of hands shall have been taken upon a question, unless a ballot thereon is so required or demanded, a declaration by the chairman of the meeting that the vote upon the question has been carried or carried by a particular majority or not carried and an entry to that effect in the minutes of the meeting shall be prima facie evidence of the fact without proof of the number of the votes recorded in favor or against any resolution or other proceeding in respect of the said question, and the result of the vote so taken shall be the decision of shareholders upon the said question.

8.18 Ballots: On any question proposed for consideration at a meeting of shareholders, a shareholder, proxyholder or other person entitled to vote may demand and the chairman may require that a ballot be taken either before or upon the declaration of the result of any vote by show of hands. If a ballot is demanded on the election of a chairman or on the question of an adjournment it shall be taken forthwith without an adjournment. A ballot demanded or required on any other question shall be taken in such manner as the chairman shall direct. A demand or requirement for a ballot may be withdrawn at any time prior to the taking of the ballot. If a ballot is taken each person present shall be entitled, in respect to the shares that he is entitled to vote at the meeting upon the question, to the number of votes as provided for by the articles or, in the absence of such provision in the articles, to one vote for each share he is entitled to vote. The result of the ballot so taken shall be the decision of the shareholders upon the question.

8.19 Adjournment: The chairman at a meeting of shareholders may, with the consent of the meeting and subject to such conditions as the meeting may decide, adjourn the meeting from time to time and from place to place. If a meeting of shareholders is adjourned for less than 30 days, it shall not be necessary to give notice of the adjourned meeting, other than by announcement at the time of the adjournment. Subject to the Act, if a meeting of shareholders is adjourned by one or more adjournments for an aggregate of 30 days or more, notice of the adjourned meeting shall be given in the same manner as notice for an original meeting.

8.20 Resolution in Lieu of a Meeting: Notwithstanding any of the foregoing provisions of this by-law a resolution in writing either ordinary or special signed by all the shareholders entitled to vote on that resolution at a meeting of shareholders is as valid as if it had been passed at a meeting of the shareholders.

11

SAMPLE #12 — Continued

8.21 Only One Shareholder: Where the Corporation has only one shareholder or only one holder of any class or series of shares, that shareholder present in person or duly represented constitutes a meeting.

Division Nine
SHARES

9.01 Allotment and Issuance: Subject to Section 25 of the Act, the articles and any unanimous shareholder agreement, the board may from time to time allot or grant options to purchase the whole or any part, including fractional parts of the authorized and unissued shares of the Corporation at such times and to such persons and for such consideration as the board shall determine, provided that no share shall be issued until it is fully paid as provided by the Act.

9.02 Commissions: The board may from time to time authorize the Corporation to pay a reasonable commission to any person in consideration of his purchasing or agreeing to purchase shares of the Corporation, whether from the Corporation or from any other person, or procuring or agreeing to procure purchasers for any such shares.

9.03 Non-Recognition of Trusts: Subject to the Act, the Corporation may treat the registered holder of any share as the person exclusively entitled to vote, to receive notices, to receive any dividend or other payments in respect of the share, and otherwise to exercise all the rights and powers of an owner of the share.

9.04 Certificates: Share certificates and the form of stock transfer power on the reverse side thereof shall (subject to the Provisions of the Act) be in such form as the board of directors may by resolution approve and such certificates shall be signed manually by the chairman of the board, or the president, or the vice-president, or the secretary, or by on behalf of a registrar, transfer agent or branch transfer agent of the Corporation, if any. The corporate seal, if any, need not be impressed upon a share certificate issued by the Corporation.

9.05 Replacement of Share Certificates: The board or any officer or agent designated by the board may in its or his discretion direct the issue of a new share or other such certificate in lieu of and upon cancellation of a certificate that has been mutilated or in substitution for a certificate claimed to have been lost, destroyed or wrongfully taken on payment of such reasonable fee and on such terms as to indemnity, reimbursement of expenses and evidence of loss and of title as the board may from time to time prescribe, whether generally or in any particular case.

9.06 Joint Holders: If two or more persons are registered as joint holders of any share, the Corporation shall not be bound to issue more than one certificate in respect thereof, and delivery of such certificate to one of such persons shall be sufficient to all of them. Any one of such persons may give effectual receipts for the certificate issued in respect thereof or for any dividend, bonus, return of capital or other money payable or warrant issuable in respect of such share.

Division Ten
TRANSFER OF SECURITIES

10.01 Registration of Transfer: Subject to the Act, no transfer of a share shall be registered in a securities register except upon presentation of the certificate representing such share with an endorsement which complies with the Act made thereon or delivered therewith duly executed by an appropriate person as provided by the Act, together with such reasonable assurance that the endorsement is genuine and effective as the board may from time to time prescribe, upon payment of all applicable taxes and any reasonable fees prescribed by the board and upon compliance with such restrictions on transfer as are authorized by the articles and upon satisfaction of any lien referred to in Section 10.04.

10.02 Transfer Agents and Registrars: The board may from time to time by resolution appoint or remove one or more transfer agents registered under the Trust Companies Act to maintain a central securities register or registers and one or more branch transfer agents to maintain branch securities register or registers. A transfer agent or branch transfer agent so appointed may be designated as such or may be designated as a registrar, according to his functions, and a person may be appointed and designed with the functions of both registrar and transfer or branch transfer agent. The board may provide for the registration of transfers of securities by and in the offices of such transfer, or branch transfer agents or registrars. In the event of any such appointment in respect of any of the shares of the Corporation, all share certificates issued by the Corporation in respect to those shares shall be countersigned by on behalf of one of the said transfer agents, branch transfer agents or registrars, if any, as the case may be.

12

SAMPLE #12 — Continued

10.03 Securities Registers: A central securities register of the Corporation shall be kept at the designated records office of the Corporation, if any, otherwise the registered office of the Corporation, or at an office or offices of a corporation or corporations registered under the Trust Companies Act as may from time to time be designated by resolution of the board of directors to act as the Corporation's transfer agent or agents. Branch securities register or registers may be kept either in or outside Alberta at such office or offices of the Corporation as the directors may determine, or at the office or offices of such other person or persons or corporations as may from time to time be designated by the resolution of the directors to act as the Corporation's branch transfer agent or agents. A branch securities register shall contain particulars of securities issued or transferred at that branch. Particulars of each issue or transfer of a security registered in a branch securities register shall also be kept in the corresponding central securities register.

10.04 Deceased Shareholders: In the event of the death of a holder, or of one of the joint holders, of any share, the Corporation shall not be required to make any entry in the securities register in respect thereof or to make any dividend or other payments in respect thereof except upon production of all such documents as may be required by law and upon compliance with the reasonable requirements of the Corporation and its transfer agents.

10.05 Lien for Indebtedness: If the articles provide that the Corporation shall have a lien on shares registered in the name of a shareholder indebted to the Corporation for any unpaid amount owing on a share issued by the Corporation on the date the Corporation was continued under the Act, such lien may be enforced, subject to the articles and to any unanimous shareholder agreement, by the sale of the shares thereby affected or by any other action, suit, remedy or proceeding authorized or permitted by law or by equity and, pending such enforcement, the Corporation may refuse to register a transfer of the whole or any part of such shares.

10.06 Alteration of share capital: Subject to the provisions of the Act, the Corporation may, by resolution of the board or of the members:

(a) increase the maximum price or consideration for which shares without nominal or par value may be issued, where such maximum price or consideration has been stated in the articles;

(b) cancel shares which, at the date of the passing of the above-mentioned resolution, have not been taken or agreed to be taken by any person, and diminish the amount of its share capital by the number of shares cancelled;

(c) cancel paid-up shares which are surrendered to the Corporation by way of gift and, if the resolution so provides, diminish the amount of its share capital by the number of shares cancelled;

(d) cancel paid-up shares that are acquired by the Corporation on a distribution of the assets of another company under liquidation proceedings, and, if the resolution so provides, diminish the amount of its share capital by the number of shares cancelled.

Division Eleven

DIVIDENDS AND RIGHTS

11.01 Dividends: Subject to the Act, the board may from time to time declare dividends payable to the shareholders according to their respective rights and interest in the Corporation. dividends may be paid in money or property or by issuing fully paid shares of the Corporation.

11.02 Dividend Cheques: A dividend payable in money shall be paid by cheque to the order of each registered holder of shares of the class or series in respect of which it has been declared, and mailed by prepaid ordinary mail to such registered holder at his address recorded in the Corporation's securities register or registers unless such holder otherwise directs. In the case of joint holders the cheque shall, unless such joint holders otherwise direct, be made payable to the order of all such joint holders and mailed to them at their recorded address. The mailing of such cheque as aforesaid, unless the same is not paid on due presentation, shall satisfy and discharge the liability for the dividend to the extent of the sum represented thereby plus the amount of any tax which the Corporation is required to and does withhold.

11.03 Non-Receipt of Cheques: In the event of non-receipt of any dividend cheque by the person to whom it is sent as aforesaid, the Corporation shall issue to such person a replacement cheque for a like amount on such terms as to indemnity, reimbursement of expenses and evidence of non-receipt and of title as the board may from time to time prescribe, whether generally or in any particular case.

11.04 Unclaimed Dividends: Any dividend unclaimed after a period of 2 years from the date of which the same has been declared to be payable shall be forfeited and shall revert to the Corporation.

13

11.05 Record Date for Dividends and Rights: The board may fix in advance a date, preceding by not more than 50 days the date for the payment of any dividend or the date for the issue of any warrant or other evidence of the right to subscribe for securities of the Corporation, as a record date for the determination of the persons entitled to receive payment of such dividend or to exercise the right to subscribe for such securities, and notice of any such record date shall be given not less than 7 days before such record date in the manner provided by the Act. If no record date is so fixed, the record date for the determination of the persons entitled to receive payment of any dividend or to exercise the right to subscribe for securities of the Corporation shall be at the close of business on the day on which the resolution relating to such dividend or right to subscribe is passed by the board.

11.06 Deduction from Dividends Payable: The Corporation may deduct from the dividends payable to any member all such sums of money as may be due from him to the Corporation on account of debts, obligations or otherwise.

Division Twelve

INFORMATION AVAILABLE TO SHAREHOLDERS

12.01 Except as provided by the Act and in paragraph 12.02 no shareholder shall be entitled to obtain information respecting any details or conduct of the Corporation's business which in the opinion of the directors would be inexpedient in the interests of the Corporation to communicate to the public.

12.02 The directors may from time to time, subject to rights conferred by the Act, determine whether and to what extent and at what time and place and under what conditions or regulations the documents, books and registers and accounting records of the Corporation or any of them shall be open to the inspection of shareholders and no shareholder shall have any right to inspect any document or book or register or account record of the Corporation except as conferred by statute or authorized by the board of directors or by a resolution of the shareholders.

Division Thirteen

NOTICES

13.01 Method of Giving Notices: Any notice or other document required by the Act, the Regulations, the articles or the by-laws to be sent to any shareholder or director or to the auditor shall be delivered personally or sent by prepaid mail or by telegram or cable or telex to any such shareholder at his latest address as shown in the records of the Corporation or its transfer agent and to any such director at his latest address as shown in the records of the Corporation or in the last notice filed under Section 101 or 108 of the Act, and to the auditor at his business address. A notice shall be deemed to be given when it is delivered personally to any such person or to his address as aforesaid; a notice mailed shall be deemed to have been given when deposited in a post office or public letter box; and a notice sent by any means of transmitted or recorded communication shall be deemed to have been given when dispatched or delivered to the appropriate communication company or agency or its representative for dispatch. The secretary may change or cause to be changed the recorded address of any shareholder, director, officer, auditor or member of a committee of the board in accordance with any information believed by him to be reliable.

13.02 Notice to Joint Shareholders: If two or more persons are registered as joint holders of any share, any notice may be addressed to all of such joint holders but notice addressed to one of such persons shall be sufficient notice to all of them.

13.03 Persons Entitled by Death or Operation of Law: Every person who, by operation of law, transfer, death of a shareholder or any other means whatsoever, shall become entitled to any share, shall be bound by every notice in respect of such share which shall have been duly given to the shareholder from whom he derives his title to such share prior to his name and address being entered on the securities register (whether such notice was given before or after the happening of the event upon which he became so entitled) and prior to his furnishing to the Corporation the proof of authority or evidence of his entitlement prescribed by the Act.

13.04 Non-Receipt of Notices: If a notice or document is sent to a shareholder by prepaid mail in accordance with Section 13.01 and the notice or document is returned on two consecutive occasions, it shall not be necessary to send any further notice or document to the shareholder until he informs the Corporation in writing of his new address; provided, always, that the return of a notice of a shareholders' meeting mailed to a shareholder in accordance with Section 13.01 of this by-law shall be deemed to be received by the shareholder on the date deposited in the mail notwithstanding the return of the notice.

13.05 Ommissions and Errors: The accidental omission to give any notice to any shareholder, director, officer, auditor or member of a committee of the board or the non-receipt of any notice by any such person or any error in any notice not affecting the substance thereof shall not invalidate any action taken at any meeting held pursuant to such notice or otherwise founded thereon.

14

SAMPLE #12 — Continued

13.06 Signature on Notices: Unless otherwise specifically provided, the signature of any director or officer of the Corporation to any notice or document to be given by the Corporation may be written, stamped, typewritten or printed or partly written, stamped, typewritten or printed.

13.07 Waiver of Notice: Any shareholder, proxyholder, other person entitled to attend a meeting of shareholders, director, officer, auditor or member of a committee of the board may at any time waive any notice, or waive or abridge the time for any notice, required to be given to him under the Act, the Regulations thereunder, the articles, the by-laws or otherwise and such waiver or abridgement, whether given before or after the meeting or other event of which notice is required to be given, shall cure any default in the giving or in the time of such notice, as the case may be. Any such waiver or abridgement shall be in writing except a waiver of notice of a meeting of shareholders or of the board of a committee of the board which may be given in any manner.

13.08 Certification of Notice: A certificate of a duly authorized person as to the facts in relation to the giving of any notice shall be prima facie evidence thereof.

13.09 Computation of Time: In computing the date when notice must be given under any provision requiring a specified number of days notice of any meeting or other event, the date of giving of the notice shall be excluded and the date of the meeting or other event shall be included.

Division Fourteen

MISCELLANEOUS

14.01 Financial Year: Until changed by the board, the financial year of the Corporation shall end on the last day of _____ , in each year.

14.02 Directors to Require Surrender of Share Certificates: The directors in office when the Certificate of Continuance is issued under the Act are hereby authorized to require the shareholders of the Corporation to surrender their share certificates, or such of their share certificates as the directors may determine, for the purpose of cancelling the share certificates and replacing them with new share certificates that comply with the Act, in particular, replacing existing share certificates with share certificates that are not negotiable securities under the Act. The directors in office shall act by resolution under this section and shall in their discretion decide the manner in which they shall require the surrender of existing share certificates and the time within which the shareholders must comply with the requirement and the form or forms of the share certificates to be issued in place of the existing share certificates. The directors may take such proceedings as they deem necessary to compel any shareholder to comply with a requirement to surrender his share certificate or certificates pursuant to this section. Notwithstanding any other provision of this by-law, but subject to the Act, the directors may refuse to register the transfer of shares represented by a share certificate that has not been surrendered pursuant to a requirement under this section.

14.03 Shareholders' Approval to Amend By-Law No. 1: The directors shall not, without the prior approval of the shareholders entitled to vote at an annual meeting of the Corporation, given by ordinary resolution, amend or repeal any provision of this by-law.

14.04 Effective Date: This by-law shall come into force upon the issue of the Certificate of Incorporation under the Act.

14.05 Unanimous Shareholder Agreement: The provisions of the by-laws shall in all respects be subject to the terms of any unanimous shareholder agreement and every director and officer shall comply therewith, and a notice thereof shall be conspicuously placed on every certificate for shares in the Corporation.

ENACTED this _____ day of _____ , 19 ____ .

_____   _____
President   Secretary

15

Company SKYWALK RESTAURANT LTD.

SHARE CERTIFICATE

Class A   No. of Shares   Par Value

Certificate # ....

Registered Name ....

Date entered in ....
Register of Members   19 ....

TRANSFER DETAILS

From: ....

To: ....

Received (Certificate Number)
this .... day of .... 19 ....

NO. A-1

INCORPORATED UNDER THE LAW OF THE PROVINCE OF ALBERTA

SHARES

SPECIMEN ONLY

This is to Certify that
is a registered holder of ....
CLASS A COMMON VOTING
fully paid and non-assessable Common shares of

with   par value

Restrictions on Transfer. There are restrictions on the right to transfer the said shares
and a copy of the full text thereof is obtainable on demand and without fee from the corporation.

IN WITNESS WHEREOF the corporation has caused this Certificate to be signed by its duly

authorized officers this .... day of .... , 19 ....

NON-NEGOTIABLE

SAMPLE #14
CLASS B SHARE CERTIFICATE

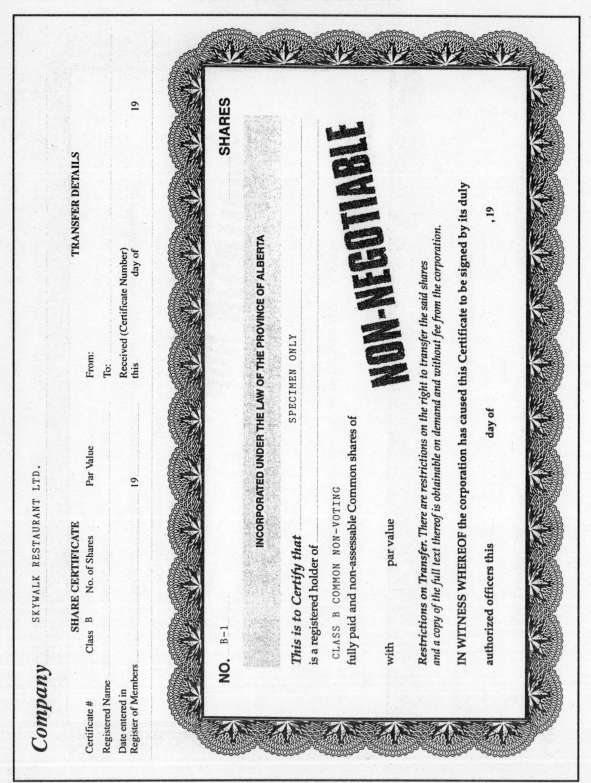

Company SKYWALK RESTAURANT LTD.

SHARE CERTIFICATE

Class B   No. of Shares   Par Value

Certificate #

Registered Name

Date entered in
Register of Members   19

TRANSFER DETAILS

From:

To:

Received (Certificate Number)
this .... day of 19

SHARES

NO. B–1

INCORPORATED UNDER THE LAW OF THE PROVINCE OF ALBERTA

SPECIMEN ONLY

NON-NEGOTIABLE

This is to Certify that
is a registered holder of

CLASS B COMMON NON–VOTING
fully paid and non-assessable Common shares of

with   par value

*Restrictions on Transfer. There are restrictions on the right to transfer the said shares
and a copy of the full text thereof is obtainable on demand and without fee from the corporation.*

IN WITNESS WHEREOF the corporation has caused this Certificate to be signed by its duly

authorized officers this   day of   , 19

SAMPLE #15
CLASS E SHARE CERTIFICATE

Company SKYWALK RESTAURANT LTD.

SHARE CERTIFICATE

Certificate # Class E No. of Shares Par Value

Registered Name

Date entered in 19
Register of Members.

TRANSFER DETAILS

From:

To:

Received (Certificate Number)
this _____ day of _____ 19

SHARES

NO. E-1

INCORPORATED UNDER THE LAW OF THE PROVINCE OF ALBERTA

SPECIMEN ONLY

This is to Certify that
is a registered holder of _____
CLASS E PREFERRED, PRIORITY TO DIVIDENDS, ENTITLED TO 12% DIVIDEND PER ANNUM, CUMULATIVE, NON-VOTING,
fully paid and non-assessable Common shares of

with _____ par value

NON-NEGOTIABLE

Restrictions on Transfer. There are restrictions on the right to transfer the said shares and a copy of the full text thereof is obtainable on demand and without fee from the corporation.

IN WITNESS WHEREOF the corporation has caused this Certificate to be signed by its duly

authorized officers this _____ day of _____ , 19

SAMPLE #16
SECURITIES REGISTER

REGISTER OF MEMBERS

OF <u>SKYWALK RESTAURANT LTD.</u>

FULL NAME	ADDRESS	OCCUPATION	DATE WHEN ENTERED AS A MEMBER	DATE WHEN CEASED TO BE A MEMBER	REPRESENTATIVE CAPACITY (IF ANY)
Stew Cooke	112 Eat Hardy Drive SW, Calgary Alberta Z1P OGO	Restauranteur	May 1/9-		Director & President
Carmel Cooke	112 Eat Hardy Drive SW, Calgary Alberta Z1P OGO	Manageress	May 1/9-		Secretary
E.T. Hardy	690 Tubby Avenue Calgary, Alberta Z1P OGO	Businessman	May 1/9-		member only

SAMPLE #17
SHAREHOLDERS' LEDGER

NAME _____ STEW COOKE _____

ADDRESS _____ 112 Eat Hardy Drive S.W. _____

_____ Calgary, Alberta Z1P OGO _____

OCCUPATION _____ Restaurateur _____

CLASS AND NOMINAL AMOUNT_ CLASS A COMMON VOTING

OF SHARES

DATE	NO. OF CERTIFICATE ISSUED	NO. OF CERTIFICATE CANCELLED	TRANSFER No.	TO OR FROM WHOM	FOLIO	PAID UP	SOLD SHARES	BOUGHT SHARES	BALANCE
May 1/9-	1A.		1	From Treasury		$100		100	100

The shareholders can, in fact, at their first meeting decide not to appoint an auditor if it is a non-distributing corporation, although this requires a unanimous shareholder resolution and is effective only on a year-to-year basis.

What do auditors do? Basically, auditors report to the shareholders on the financial statements prepared for the company. Auditors are entitled to examine any documents and receive any information that they require from the directors and officers. They report their findings to the company at the shareholders' meeting or in the financial statements they prepare, appropriately known as the "audited financial statements."

If there are any discrepancies or questions raised by an auditor, the shareholders can then demand answers or rectification by the directors. In all likelihood, in your non-distributing company, as in the case of Skywalk Restaurant Ltd., the appointment of an auditor will not be necessary.

5. Banking documents

All banking or financial institutions require the board of directors to pass resolutions which authorize the opening of a corporate bank account.

At the organizational meeting, you should use the banking documents that each particular institution requires its customers to sign. In all likelihood, the documents will have to be signed by both the president and the secretary of the company. These bank documents are readily available from the institution that you will be dealing with. Although each bank and lending institution uses different documents, they all basically provide the same rights for the company and the bank.

6. Corporate seal

For many people, one of the great pleasures of incorporating a company is the acquisition and use of a corporate seal. Although historically a corporate seal had some use, it is not legally required under the Business Corporations Act.

However, a corporate seal may be required when you sign documents such as the banking resolutions. Therefore, you should approve the purchase of a corporate seal and obtain one (for approximately $35 to $40 per seal) mainly as a precaution so you will not run into an unnecessary delay when funding is required and you need to use the seal.

The resolution in your organizational meeting minutes should also state clearly that the president and secretary (or other officer) are fully authorized to sign documents on behalf of the company without the seal.

7. Miscellaneous

Under this heading, the company is entitled to consider a number of items. For example, Skywalk Restaurant Ltd. approved in a resolution the names of the solicitors and accountants of the company and the location of the records office and the registered office.

Another provision authorizes those who can sign general contracts on behalf of the company and repeats the fact that a corporate seal is not required to bind the company to the agreement.

One other matter should always be considered when you set up the organizational minutes. Often, prior to incorporation, the incorporator enters into a contract that is, in effect, a contract that the corporation will take over. For example, Mr. Cooke had to sign an offer to lease with the landlord of the premises where the corporation planned to open up a restaurant. Mr. Cooke could not wait until the corporation was in place so he signed the lease in his own name.

Under the Business Corporations Act, a company can adopt or ratify a contract that was entered into before its incorporation and take over the obligations and liabilities under the contract.

Once the corporation has adopted this contract, it is bound by its terms and entitled to its benefits. Upon proper notice, the other party to the contract is bound to deal with the company and not the individual who initially signed the contract. So, if you have to break the contract for some reason, the other party could not take action against you, but would have to go against the company.

The final clause in the organizational minutes is often a waiver clause where you consent to the meeting being held and waive notice of the meeting or any irregularities or informalities, such as lack of a quorum, at the meeting.

This type of waiver clause is provided for in the by-laws. It basically removes the burden of providing formal notice of the meeting and following the required formalities. A waiver clause can also be used in shareholders' meetings.

Attach to your minutes the share subscriptions, which are basically an offer from individuals who want to buy shares in the company. These provide some written evidence of each share issuance. They should be prepared, filed in the minute book, and signed by all parties who obtain shares in the company.

The organizational minutes are shown in Sample #18 and a share subscription in Sample #19.

c. FIRST SHAREHOLDERS' MEETING

A shareholders' meeting should be held shortly after the first directors' meeting so the shareholders can properly ratify some of the items resolved at the directors' meeting. Once the shareholders have been issued shares, they are entitled to attend the meeting. In the case of Skywalk Restaurant Ltd., only the Class A shareholders have the right to vote. Class B and E shareholders are entitled to attend the meeting, but they do not have any say in the passing of resolutions.

Sample #20 shows the minutes of the first shareholders' meeting of Skywalk Restaurant Ltd. At that meeting, the shareholders did the following things:

(a) Approved the appointment of the board of directors to remain in office until the first annual general meeting of the company

(b) Approved the by-laws as adopted by the directors

(c) Agreed not to appoint an auditor for the forthcoming business year (this confirms the decision of the incorporators)

As discussed before, the shareholders rely on the board of directors for the management and control of the business and have very little input into that aspect of the operation. Accordingly, these minutes can be short and sweet, and the form of waiver clause used in the directors' minutes can also be modified and used in the shareholders' minutes.

In conjunction with the preparation of the shareholders' minutes, you should complete the directors' register in the minute book. Fill in the full names, addresses, and occupations of the directors. The directors' register for Skywalk Restaurant Ltd. is shown in Sample #21.

d. SHAREHOLDER AGREEMENTS

It has become quite common for shareholders in a company to enter into a private agreement that governs such things as selling or transferring shares after a death or dispute, pooling shares to vote for certain directors, or restricting the transfer of shares in one way or another. These agreements are known as "shareholder agreements."

In situations where shareholders are "at arm's length" (in other words, not family members), shareholders' agreements can be very useful. They are internal documents between those shareholders only;

SAMPLE #18
MINUTES OF THE
ORGANIZATIONAL MEETING

MINUTES OF THE ORGANIZATIONAL MEETING OF THE FIRST DIRECTOR OF SKYWALK RESTAURANT LTD. HELD AT 112 EAT HARDY DRIVE S.W., CALGARY, ALBERTA ON THE 1ST DAY OF MAY, 199- AT THE HOUR OF 10:00 O'CLOCK IN THE FORENOON PURSUANT TO SECTION 99 OF THE BUSINESS CORPORATIONS ACT.

PRESENT:

STEW COOKE

being the sole director of the Corporation.

The sole director of the Corporation being present, Notice of the Meeting was waived.

Mr. COOKE acted as Chairman of the Meeting and as Secretary thereof.

CERTIFICATE OF INCORPORATION

The Chairman reported that the Corporation had been duly incorporated under The Business Corporations Act and produced to the Meeting Certificate of Incorporation No. 12345678 issued by the Registrar of Corporations, certifying that the Corporation had been duly incorporated under The Business Corporations Act on the 17th day of April, 199-. A duplicate original of the Articles of Incorporation of the Corporation, as registered with the Alberta Consumer and Corporate Affairs was produced and ordered to be inserted in the Minute Book of the Corporation.

APPOINTMENT OF DIRECTORS AND OFFICERS

The Chairman advised that pursuant to the terms of the Business Corporations Act Stew Cooke shall be the Director of the Corporation until the first meeting of Shareholders and accordingly is authorized to elect officers for the Corporation to hold office until the Annual Shareholders' meeting. UPON MOTION DULY MADE the following persons were elected officers of the Corporation to hold office until the Annual Shareholders' meeting:

Stew Cooke   President
Carmel Cooke   Secretary

COMPANY SEAL

UPON MOTION IT WAS UNANIMOUSLY RESOLVED that the press seal, an impress of which appears on this set of Minutes, be adopted as the common seal of the Corporation.

SHARE CERTIFICATE

UPON MOTION IT WAS UNANIMOUSLY RESOLVED that the form of share certificate attached to these Minutes be adopted as the form of share certificate for the Class A, B, and E shares of the Corporation and all restrictions on this class of share will be referred to in the share certificate.

REGISTERED OFFICE AND RECORDS ADDRESS

The Chairman of the Meeting advised that it was necessary to pass a resolution with respect to the registered office and records address of the Corporation.

UPON MOTION IT WAS UNANIMOUSLY RESOLVED that the Registered Office of the Corporation shall be 112 Eat Hardy Drive S.W., Calgary, Alberta and that all of the documents, notices and minutes required by law shall be kept at the said address as well as all Registers and the Corporate Minute Book. The books of account and accounting records of the Corporation shall not be kept at the Registered Office of the Corporation but shall be kept at 1504 Highrise Commercial Centre, 600-6th Avenue S.W., Calgary, Alberta which shall be the records address for the Corporation.

ISSUES OF SHARES

The Chairman advised the Meeting that the following subscriptions for shares had been received at the price of $1.00 per share for the Class "A" and "B" shares and $50.00 per share for the Class "E" shares:

Stew Cooke	100 Class "A"
Carmel Cooke	100 Class "B"
E.T. Hardy	50 Class "E"

UPON MOTION IT WAS UNANIMOUSLY RESOLVED that the shares subscribed for be and the same are hereby allotted and issued to the persons listed below, as fully paid and non-assessable at the price of $1.00 per share for the Class "A" and "B" shares and $50.00 per share for the Class "C" shares and that the Corporation add to its stated capital account for the Class "A" shares the sum of $100.00; Class "B" shares the sum of $100.00; and the Class "E" shares the sum of $2 500.00:

NAME	NO. & CLASS OF SHARES	PRICE PER SHARE	CERT. NO.
Stew Cooke	100 Class "A"	$1.00	-1A-
Carmel Cooke	100 Class "B"	$1.00	-1B-
E.T. Hardy	50 Class "E"	$50.00	-1E-

SOLICITORS

UPON MOTION IT WAS UNANIMOUSLY RESOLVED that the Solicitors for the Corporation be and the same are Harem and Scarem, whose offices are located at 888-88th Avenue S.W., Calgary, Alberta.

ACCOUNTANTS

UPON MOTION IT WAS UNANIMOUSLY RESOLVED that the Accountants for the Corporation be and the same are Smith and Co. Accountants.

BANKING RESOLUTIONS

UPON MOTION IT WAS UNANIMOUSLY RESOLVED that the Royal Bank at Highrise Place be appointed the bankers of the Corporation and that the resolutions and other banking documents in the forms attached hereto be and are hereby adopted as the banking resolutions and documents of the Corporation and that the President and/or Secretary are hereby authorized to sign and execute the same, where indicated.

GENERAL CONTRACTS

   UPON MOTION IT WAS UNANIMOUSLY RESOLVED THAT:

1. The president of the Corporation is hereby authorized to sign in the name and on behalf of the Corporation all instruments in writing and any instruments in writing so signed shall be binding upon the Corporation without any other formality.

2. The Board shall have power from time to time by Resolution to appoint any other officer or officers or any person or persons on behalf of the Corporation either to sign instruments in writing generally or to sign specific instruments in writing.

3. The Corporate Seal of the Corporation may when required be affixed to instruments in writing so signed as aforesaid or by any officer or officers, person or persons appointed as aforesaid by resolution of the Board.

BY-LAWS

   UPON MOTION IT WAS UNANIMOUSLY RESOLVED that By-Law Number 1 attached to these Minutes be adopted to regulate the business and affairs of the Corporation, subject to the approval by the Shareholders of the Corporation.

   There being no further business, the Meeting, ON MOTION, terminated.

APPROVED: ___*Stew Cooke*___
                Chairman

WAIVER

I, being the sole incorporator and director of the above-named Corporation, consent to the holding of this Meeting at the above time and place and I do hereby waive notice of this meeting and of any irregularities or informalities in the holding thereof and do hereby ratify, acquiesce in and confirm the business transacted by the said Meeting.

___*Stew Cooke*___
Stew Cooke

SAMPLE #19
SHARE SUBSCRIPTION

SUBSCRIPTIONS FOR SHARES

TO: SKYWALK RESTAURANT LTD.
        and the Directors thereof.

   The undersigned hereby subscribes for and agrees to take up One Hundred (100) Class "A" shares in the authorized capital of SKYWALK RESTAURANT LTD. and tenders herewith the sum of One Hundred ($100.00) Dollars in full payment of the aggregate subscription price for such shares.

   The undersigned hereby requests that the said shares be allotted to the undersigned or to such persons as the undersigned may in writing direct, that such shares be issued as fully paid and non-assessable and that a certificate representing such shares be issued in the name of the undersigned or as the undersigned may in writing direct.

                                        DATED at the City of Calgary, in the Province of Alberta, this 1st day of May, 199-.

                                        Stew Cooke
                                        STEW COOKE

SAMPLE #20
MINUTES OF THE FIRST SHAREHOLDERS' MEETING

MINUTES OF THE FIRST MEETING OF THE SHAREHOLDERS OF SKYWALK RESTAURANT LTD. HELD AT 112 EAT HARDY DRIVE S.W., CALGARY, ALBERTA ON THE 1ST DAY OF MAY, 199- AT THE HOUR OF 3:30 O'CLOCK IN THE AFTERNOON PURSUANT TO SECTION 99 OF THE BUSINESS CORPORATIONS ACT.

PRESENT:

STEW COOKE

CARMEL COOKE

E.T. HARDY

being all of the Shareholders of the Corporation.

Mr. Cooke acted as Chairman of the Meeting and Mrs. Cooke acted as Secretary thereof.

All of the shareholders being present, Notice of the Meeting was waived.

BORROWING RESOLUTION

UPON MOTION IT WAS UNANIMOUSLY RESOLVED that the banking resolution, a copy of which is attached to these Minutes, be passed thereby authorizing the directors from time to time to borrow on behalf of the Corporation and to give security therefor.

APPOINTMENT OF DIRECTORS

The Chairman then advised that it was necessary to appoint directors for the Corporation and ON MOTION DULY MADE AND SECONDED IT WAS UNANIMOUSLY RESOLVED the following were elected directors of the Corporation for the following term of office:

NAME	TERM	ADDRESS
STEW COOKE	1 year	112 Eat Hardy Dr. S.W. Calgary, Alberta

CONFIRMATION OF BY-LAWS

UPON MOTION IT WAS UNANIMOUSLY RESOLVED that the adoption of By-Law Number 1 by the sole Director of the Corporation be approved and confirmed.

SAMPLE #20 — Continued

AUDITOR

UPON MOTION IT WAS UNANIMOUSLY RESOLVED that the Company not appoint an auditor for the forthcoming year.

There being no further business, ON MOTION, the Meeting terminated.

APPROVED: _Stew Cooke_____
Chairman

WAIVER

"WE, all of the Shareholders of the above-named Company, hereby consent to the holding of this Meeting at the above time and place, and we do hereby waive notice of this Meeting and of any irregularities or informalities in the holding thereof and do hereby ratify, acquiesce in and confirm the business transacted by the said Meeting."

_Stew Cooke_____
STEW COOKE

_Carmel Cooke_____
CARMEL COOKE

_E. T. Hardy_____
E.T. HARDY

SAMPLE #21
DIRECTORS' REGISTER

REGISTER OF DIRECTORS AND MANAGERS

OF _____SKYWALK RESTAURANT LTD._____

FULL NAME	ADDRESS	OCCUPATION	DATE WHEN APPOINTED OR ELECTED	DATE WHEN CEASED TO HOLD OFFICE	POSITION HELD
Stew Cooke	112 Eat Hardy Drive SW, Calgary Alberta Z1P OGO	Restauranteur	May 1/9-		Director & President
Carmel Cooke	112 Eat Hardy Drive SW, Calgary Alberta Z1P OGO	Manageress	May 1/9-		Secretary

the corporation is usually only a passive party to the agreement.

1. Buy-sell agreements

A buy-sell agreement is one of the more common forms of shareholder agreements in use. It provides only for what happens when a shareholder dies or when one shareholder wishes to sell shares or to buy out the shares of the other shareholder. This provision, known as a shotgun clause, is very handy in settling disputes.

Shareholder agreements of this type provide mechanisms for solving disputes, especially where shares are held evenly between two or more parties and a stalemate arises.

2. Unanimous shareholder agreements

Under the terms of the Business Corporations Act, an additional advantage to having a shareholder agreement has been introduced. A *unanimous* written agreement of all the shareholders of the company can be the single most important document governing the day-to-day and long-term operations of the company. Sample #22 shows a special resolution approving a unanimous shareholder agreement.

Unanimous shareholder agreements may provide for any of the following:

(a) The regulation of the rights and liabilities of the shareholders among themselves (which basically reiterates the existing agreements used by shareholders)

(b) The election of directors

(c) The management of the business of the corporation including the restriction or abrogation in whole or in part of the powers of the directors

(d) Any other matters that the shareholders wish to include in the agreements.

Clauses (c) and (d) change the existing law by allowing the shareholders, under the unanimous shareholder agreement, to take over some or all of the powers and rights of the directors and control the company themselves. This is a significant change from the usual separation of management and ownership, but it makes sense in small non-distributing companies. Many of these companies are simply incorporated partnerships anyway, and the law is recognizing the reality that the shareholders and directors are one and the same. It is sometimes easier to operate a company using the unanimous shareholder agreement than going through the fiction of having the directors make the decisions.

However, the act does provide that the shareholders will be deemed to have the rights, powers, and, more importantly, the duties and liabilities of directors to the extent that the agreement gives them the authority that the directors had.

In Skywalk Restaurant Ltd., a unanimous shareholder agreement is not required because Mr. Cooke has sole control. The shareholders of that company are content to maintain the shareholder-director split. Similarly, they found no need for a normal shareholder or buy-sell agreement because they already agreed that Mr. Cooke will have full control over the company and that Mr. Hardy's position will be simply that of an investor.

Amendments to the unanimous shareholder agreement have to be made with the unanimous agreement of all the shareholders of the company. This requirement makes obvious sense, but it could cause problems if changes are required but minority shareholders do not want to approve them.

In contrast, amendments to the Articles of Incorporation require only a two-thirds majority and amendments to the by-laws require only a simple majority of both directors and shareholders. In many instances, the same provision can be included in any one of those three documents. The greater the majority required to amend the document, the more inflexible that particular aspect of the management of the company will be.

It is very important when preparing a unanimous shareholder agreement to include only those items that are either so important they require 100% unanimity to change or so fundamental that they would never be changed anyway.

In a situation where two or more people set up a corporation and all parties hold the same number of shares, I would strongly recommend that all parties enter a unanimous shareholders' agreement. The agreement should cover all matters relating to resolving deadlocks and making arrangements in the event of death or disability.

Recent tax changes affect agreements relating to the death of a shareholder. If you have purchased life insurance, make sure that your agreement provides for the appropriate method of collecting funds without adverse tax consequences. Legal or tax advice is recommended in this situation.

SPECIAL RESOLUTION OF THE SHAREHOLDERS
OF LAZY DAY LANDSCAPING LTD.

UNANIMOUSLY RESOLVED as a Special Resolution of the Shareholders of LAZY DAY LANDSCAPING LTD. that the Unanimous Shareholders' Agreement, a copy of which is annexed to this Resolution, be and is hereby approved and confirmed;

The Corporate Secretary is empowered to provide all shareholders with an executed copy of this Agreement duly acknowledged by the Board of Directors for and on behalf of the Company.

CERTIFIED a true copy of a Special Resolution of the Shareholders of LAZY DAY LAND-SCAPING LTD. this 20th day of July, 199-.

Lana Lazy
Lana Lazy
Secretary

5
WHAT TO DO AFTER INCORPORATION

Once your company has been properly incorporated and organized, the requirements for keeping the company in good standing are minimal as long as no major changes take place. However, in the life of a company, as in the life of an individual, growth and changes occur. This chapter tells you about some of the first things to do in your new corporation.

a. TRANSFERRING PERSONAL ASSETS TO THE COMPANY

1. Shareholders' loans

One major reason to incorporate is the protection of limited liability. In other words, a shareholder's risk is limited to the amount of the share investment in the company. In most cases, when a shareholder is incorporating a company, it is done to achieve specific goals. Almost invariably, the achievement of these goals will involve the expenditure of some cash or the use of some other valuable personal assets as part of the business. You must, therefore, decide how best to get those assets into the company.

One method would be to put all of the cash or the cash value of the assets into the company by purchasing shares. For example, Mr. Cooke personally owns $25 000 worth of kitchen equipment and a station wagon worth $5 000 that he is going to use for the business. He will also buy another $5 000 worth of equipment, including tables, chairs, etc. Therefore, if he wished, he could buy $35 000 worth of shares from the company so that each of his 100 shares would cost $350. However, the risk is that

if the company encounters financial difficulty, Mr. Cooke could lose his entire $35 000 investment.

A safer way would be for Mr. Cooke to acquire the minimum share capital that would guarantee him control and then sell or loan the balance of his assets to the company. Note that Mr. Hardy is buying Class E shares at $50 per share. He is investing in the company. If the company gets into trouble, he could lose his $50 per share investment.

As Mr. Cooke has no cash to put into the company, he will use a rollover procedure that is discussed below. However, Mrs. Cooke has $5 000 cash that she wants to contribute to the company. How can she best do this?

The $5 000 cash can be put into the company as a shareholder's loan. Any time a shareholder or third party puts something into a company, the company should give back some form of consideration. If the company does not do so, there will be no legal way to recover what has been put in. In other words, Mrs. Cooke can give $5 000 to the company without taking back any form of security, but if the company suffers financial difficulty she could lose her $5 000.

The better method is to lend the money to the company and take back at least a promissory note and perhaps some other security. A simple promissory demand note provides evidence that the monies were lent to the company by Mrs. Cooke and that upon demand Mrs. Cooke can force the company to repay her the funds.

Sample #23 shows the promissory note given by the company to Mrs. Cooke. The promissory note is payable 60 days after demand. The deadline for payment is designed to minimize the tax consequences for both parties. The promissory note also includes a repayment of interest to Mrs. Cooke at the rate of 12% per annum "both before and after maturity." This means that after demand, interest at the rate of 12% will still be owed by the company until the date of payment.

Being a cautious individual, Mrs. Cooke has asked for some additional security from the company besides the promissory note. She is aware that if the company gets into financial difficulty, although she will be able to call upon the company to satisfy the terms of the note, she would still be considered an unsecured creditor. She will share with all other unsecured creditors in picking the bones of the company after all of the other secured creditors have removed most of the meat.

She wants to be a secured creditor, so the company has agreed to give her security on some of the assets that the company acquires. Specifically, the company has agreed to give her a "Security Agreement" worth $5 000 over some of the kitchen equipment. This Agreement must be registered at the Personal Property Security Registry in Alberta through the use of a private registry office. If the company defaults in repaying Mrs. Cooke the $5 000 plus interest, she will have the right to have the kitchen equipment seized and sold. The proceeds will be used first to pay off the costs of the seizure and second to pay her. In other words, Mrs. Cooke now has a secure position and will have a priority on the return of her monies plus interest, at least to the extent of the value of the security that she has taken. Security agreements are explained in more detail in chapter 9.

If you want to acquire security from your company, I suggest that you get legal advice because many of the laws in this area have recently changed. See chapter 9 for a more detailed review of the types of security that a company can provide to creditors.

2. Rollovers

Mr. Cooke could also sell his assets to the company and secure them in a manner similar to Mrs. Cooke's procedure. However, it becomes slightly more complicated when dealing with assets other than cash because tax consequences must be considered.

A sale of an asset from one legal entity to another entity is called a disposition for purposes of income tax law. If the asset is sold for more than it cost, a capital gain will be incurred by the selling party. Similarly, if the selling party has depreciated the asset to a point where its book value is less than the selling price, not only is there a possibility of a capital gain but also a "recapture" of some income.

This rule would make it difficult and, in fact, prohibitive for you to sell assets to your company. However, since one of the underlying philosophies of our tax laws is to encourage business to be done through corporations, the Income Tax Act allows some assets to be "rolled over" into a company tax free as long as certain procedures are followed. Do not get the impression that the tax department is offering a windfall; the rollover legislation ensures that if the individual does not have to pay taxes on the rollover of the asset, the company will eventually have to do so on the sale of that asset.

At any rate, the rollover, commonly known as a section 85 rollover, works as follows:

(a) First, determine which assets you will rollover into the company. Only assets worth more at the time of the proposed rollover should be transferred in this way. Section 85 rollovers cover most assets, such as shares, equipment, vehicles, bonds,

SAMPLE #23
PROMISSORY NOTE

PROMISSORY NOTE

Calgary, Alberta
May 2, 199-
$5 000.00

FOR VALUE RECEIVED, the undersigned does hereby promise unconditionally to pay to the order of Carmel Cooke the sum of Five Thousand ($5,000.00) Dollars sixty (60) days after demand plus interest thereon at the rate of 12% per annum calculated both before and after payment.

THE MAKER AND ENDORSER of this Note does hereby waive notice of protest and dishonor.

DATED at the City of Calgary, in the Province of Alberta, this 2nd day of May, 199-.

SKYWALK RESTAURANT LTD.

Per: *Stew Cooke*

lands purchased as an investment, goodwill, incorporation costs, and inventory. Section 85 excludes inventory of real property.

(b) Determine the fair market value of the assets.

(c) Determine the "elected price"; this price will normally be the price that the seller originally paid for the asset or the original value of the asset.

(d) Prepare and sign a rollover agreement between you and your company.

(e) File the election forms with Revenue Canada at the same time as you file your personal or computer tax returns (whichever you do first).

I have simplified the process for purposes of illustration only. The determination of either (b) or (c) may be a difficult one. If problems arise, discuss this matter with your accountant before proceeding.

Your agreement should include what is known as a price adjustment clause, which will allow you to adjust your values if the tax department claims that you have improperly valued the assets.

The most important aspect of the rollover procedure is that the assets are sold to the company and the company gives back to the seller a promissory note for the asset value up to the "elected price" of the asset and preferred shares for the difference between the elected price and the fair market value. For example, if the fair market value of the assets that Mr. Cooke is selling to the company is set at $35 000 and the agreed value has been set at $20 000, the company will give Mr. Cooke a promissory note payable on demand with interest for $20 000 and $15 000 worth of Class E preferred shares. The shares should specify both an "issue" price (for purposes of determining the stated capital) and a "redemption" price

representing the price payable to Mr. Cooke should the company wish to repurchase some or all of those preferred shares.

It is important to give Mr. Cooke preferred shares rather than common shares in order to avoid the problem of a deemed gift to the other shareholders. In other words, if Mr. Cooke received common shares, the tax department could take the position that not only Mr. Cooke, but also Mrs. Cooke and perhaps even Mr. Hardy benefited from the additional assets that the company acquired. By giving Mr. Cooke preferred shares, he has been given a preference to the repayment, so the other shareholders have not received a deemed gift.

Sample #24 shows a sample section 85 rollover agreement between the company and Mr. Cooke. There are many variations to the way the section 85 rollover agreement can be set up. Some professional advice is necessary to structure it properly. In addition to the agreement, election forms (Form T2056) have to be filed with the tax department in a timely manner to properly effect the rollover. Again, I recommend that you seek legal or accounting assistance in the preparation of the section 85 rollover documents to ensure that the paperwork and filings are done properly.

3. Capital gains

If you have been carrying on business as a sole proprietor and now wish to incorporate, it is quite possible that many of your assets have increased in value from the time that you acquired them.

A tax-free capital gains exemption is available on the transfer of farmland and shares of an active small business into a corporation. If you are lucky enough to own assets in either category, I recommend that you take advantage of this rollover while it is still available. Because the paperwork must be precise, you must get proper legal and accounting advice.

THIS AGREEMENT made effective this 2nd day of May, 199-

BETWEEN:

STEW COOKE ("the Vendor")
— and —
SKYWALK RESTAURANT LTD. ("the Purchaser")

AGREEMENT

WHEREAS the Vendor is the owner of certain properties as listed on Schedule "A" attached hereto ("the Property").

AND WHEREAS the Vendor desires to sell and the Purchaser desires to purchase the Property.

NOW THEREFORE the parties agree as follows:

1. The Vendor hereby sells and the Purchaser hereby purchases the property listed on Schedule "A" attached hereto for an amount equal to the fair market value of the property which the parties agree is as set out in Schedule "A" attached hereto, under or opposite the description "FMV" and the purchase price shall be allocated to the various assets and classes of assets as set out in Schedule "A."

2. The parties hereby agree that the intent of the sale herein is the transfer of the property set out in Schedule "A" at an elected amount from the Vendor to the Purchaser in accordance with the provisions of Section 85 of the Income Tax Act of Canada and accordingly the Vendor and Purchaser shall jointly elect under that section that the elected amount for the property by this Agreement sold to the Purchaser shall be the amount or amounts set out in Schedule "A" for each item of property sold under or opposite the description "elected amount."

3. The purchase price shall be paid by the Purchaser as follows:

(a) By non-interest bearing Demand Promissory Note in the amount of $20 000.00.

(b) By issue to the Vendor of 50 shares in the capital stock of the Purchaser
under the following additional terms and conditions:

 (i) The shares shall be Class "E" shares.

 (ii) The shares shall have an aggregate issue value of $50.00 per share.

 (iii) The shares shall have their total aggregate premium for redemption
 set at $15 000.00.

 (iv) The cumulative cash dividend percentage for the share shall be 12%.

 (v) The number of shares issued will be set out in Schedule "A" under or
 opposite the description "Pref. Shares."

4. The vendor warrants that all assets herein sold are as at the effective date above described free and clear of all mortgages, encumbrances, charges, and other third party rights of any nature or kind whatsoever except as herein set out as obligations to be assumed by the Purchaser.

5. The Parties covenant and agree with each other that they will from time to time at the request of the other execute and deliver all of such additional instruments, notices, releases, and other documents and shall do all other acts and things as may be necessary to carry out the purpose of this agreement.

6. This paragraph shall be effective, and all amendments to the amounts payable by cash or note, the amount of the redemption amount for shares in the nature of preference shares agreed to be issued, the purchase price and the elected amount herein required shall be made in the event that the Department of National Revenue, pursuant to the provisions of the Income Tax Act, or any provincial taxing authority, pursuant to a provincial taxing Statute, shall rule or determine with all appeals dismissed or abandoned that any of the fair market values, undepreciated capital costs for depreciable property or cost amounts for non-depreciable property, fair market values of cash, notes payable or indebtedness assumed, fair market values of shares issued or fair market values of assets purchased and sold are other than they have been agreed to in this Agreement.

7. The effective date of the purchase and sale herein agreed to shall be as first above written and the parties specifically agree and acknowledge that this written agreement is the written memorandum of and verbal agreement previously entered into on or before the effective date and accordingly, effective as at the date first above written although not executed by the parties until the date indicated where the signatures and seals of the various parties appear.

8. All periodic payments required to be made in respect of the property herein purchased and sold and that are normally subject to adjustment as between a Vendor and a Purchaser, including but not limited to taxes, maintenance, fees, and insurance payments, shall be paid by the Vendors up to the effective date of this Agreement and thereafter by the purchaser and all necessary adjustments shall be made in cash between the vendor and the Purchaser forthwith upon the execution of this Agreement.

9. This Agreement shall enure to the benefit of and be binding upon the parties hereto together with their respective heirs, executors, administrators, successors, and assigns.

IN WITNESS WHEREOF, the parties have executed this Agreement on the dates below indicated.

SIGNED, SEALED AND DELIVERED before me this 2nd day of April 199-

Stew Cooke

STEW COOKE

J. M. Witness Witness

SIGNED, SEALED AND DELIVERED by a proper officer of the Company, in that behalf this 2nd day of April 199-

SKYWALK RESTAURANT LTD.

Per: *Stew Cooke*

Per: *Carmel Cooke*

This is Schedule "A" to the Agreement between Stew Cooke ("the Vendor") and Skywalk Restaurant Ltd. ("the Purchaser") made effective this 2nd day of May, 199-.

ASSET SOLD	FAIR MARKET VALUE	ELECTED AMOUNT	NO. OF PREFERRED SHARES
Industrial ovens			
Serial No. 86712	$10 000.00	$8 000.00	6.25
Tables and chairs,			
utensil sets	$5 000.00	$2 000.00	18.75
Microwave ovens			
Serial No. 12345P	$20 000.00	$10 000.00	25
Serial No. 8765M			
Serial No. 14790			
	$35 000.00	$20 000.00	50

*Each preferred share shall have an issue price of $1.00 per share and a redemption price of $300.00 per share.

b. MISCELLANEOUS MATTERS THAT MAY ARISE IN THE DAY-TO-DAY OPERATIONS OF YOUR COMPANY

What follows is a discussion of some areas that may require changes to your corporate structure from time to time. These items apply to companies that have been incorporated under the Business Corporations Act.

When requesting corporate services, use the Request for Corporate Services form supplied free of charge by the Corporate Registry (see Sample #25).

1. Change of name

At any time, a company may change its name simply by passing a special resolution and having the name approved by the Companies Branch. The name approval process is identical to the process discussed in chapter 3. Consents or undertaking to dissolve within six months of the consent may be required from existing companies with a similar name.

The filing fee for a change of name is $75. Because the effect of a change of name is to amend the Articles of Incorporation, Articles of Amendment should be filled out and submitted to the Companies Branch.

As an example, assume that Skywalk Restaurant Ltd. wishes to change its name to Highrise Restaurants Ltd. The necessary Articles of Amendment are shown in Sample #26. Because there is a company in Alberta with the name of High Ways Restaurants Ltd., a consent from that company is also required (see Sample #27).

Under the Business Corporations Act, a change of a company name can be deemed to be a "fundamental change." This can trigger certain special shareholders' rights, which are discussed later in this chapter.

2. Change of directors, registered office, or records office

Directors of a company are normally elected on a year-to-year basis. The shareholders may increase the number of directors by electing new directors in a shareholders' resolution.

The directors have the right under most by-laws to appoint replacement directors if there is a resignation or death. This can be done in a resolution of the board of directors.

The removal of directors may, subject to a unanimous shareholder agreement, be carried out by the shareholders in an ordinary resolution at a special meeting called by the shareholders for that purpose. A director is entitled to receive notice and attend the meeting to defend himself or herself.

Within 15 days of any change in the directorship, the company must send to the Registrar a notice of the changes, to be filed at the Companies Branch. Form 6 doubles as a Notice of Directors and a Notice of Change of Directors.

Remember that the Canadian residency requirements will apply at all times, so if you are changing directors, make sure that at least a majority of the directors are resident Canadians.

Sample #28 shows a special resolution of Highrise Restaurants Ltd. electing Mrs. Cooke to the board of directors. Sample #29 shows Form 6, which reports this change.

A company is also entitled to change its records office or registered office from time to time as long as the new offices meet the requirements discussed earlier. A directors' resolution is required to make those changes. The corporation is required to send a notice of that change to the Companies Branch within 15 days. Use Form 3, which is the same Notice of Address form used before.

Assume that Mr. Cooke's business is booming, so he sells his house and moves into a better neighborhood. He has to change the registered office of the company. Sample #30 shows the appropriate directors' resolution and Sample #31 shows Form 3, which is submitted to the Companies Branch.

3. Dividends

Dividends are the magic word in determining whether or not a company has been profitable. If, at the end of the corporate year, there are sufficient retained earnings in the company to allow for a distribution of some funds, they may be paid out as dividends.

Monies can be paid out to those involved in the company in many different ways, including employment income, directors' bonuses, and repayment of loans. However, dividends are paid to shareholders for no reason other than the fact that they are shareholders and are entitled to share in the profits of the company.

The board of directors must be extremely cautious when declaring dividends. A company is not entitled to pay dividends if there are reasonable grounds to believe that after payment of those dividends the company will be unable to pay its debts or that the "realizable value" of the company's assets will be less than the total of its liability and stated capital.

These solvency tests have been designed to ensure that creditors of the company are not taken advantage of by having a company pay dividends to its shareholders when the company is really not in a position to do so.

There are different types of dividends that a corporation can declare. The distinction is based on where those monies come from. For example, if the monies are earned in the active business of the company, the tax treatment of the dividends will be different than if the monies are earned in passive investments, such as term deposits and ownership of share portfolios. Capital gains made by the company on the sale of a capital asset may be given out to shareholders as dividends in yet a third way.

This distinction is significant because, depending on the type of dividend that is declared, both the company and the individual receiving the dividend will have different tax consequences to deal with. In order to ensure that the tax consequences are minimized, consult with your accountant or bookkeeper.

The declaration of a dividend is the responsibility of the directors who, assuming the company has met the solvency requirements stated above, can declare dividends in a directors' resolution.

In making this decision, the directors will have to make sure that there is enough money left in the company for contingencies and for operating capital, because the company will not be able to borrow monies and then pay a dividend with those funds.

As well, the directors will have to ensure that if any dividends are paid, they are paid first to the preferred shareholders, if any, and then, if any monies are left, to the common shareholders.

In the case of Highrise Restaurants Ltd., the directors decided that there were sufficient monies to pay a dividend to the preferred shareholders but not to the common shareholders. Accordingly, Sample #32 shows a directors' resolution issuing a dividend of $10 per share on all the Class E preferred shares. This gives Mr. Hardy some dividend income amounting to a 20% return on his investment (because he paid $50 per share initially). Mr. Cooke also receives some dividend income from the preferred shares that he acquired in the section 85 rollover agreement discussed earlier.

There are no filing requirements with the Companies Branch when your company declares dividends. There may be some filings necessary for income tax purposes; you should consult with your accountant or bookkeeper to find out any requirements in that area.

SAMPLE #25
REQUEST FOR CORPORATE SERVICES

Alberta
REGISTRIES

PO Box 1007
Stn Main
Edmonton Alberta
T5J 4W6

IMPORTANT
Please read the instructions
on the back of this form

Request For Services

FOR CASH REGISTER USE ONLY

Date of Request

1.

Your File Number	Name of Company - Existing or Proposed (for which services are required)	Amount	Corporate Access Number (if known)

2. Name

Address   (Street)

          (City, Province)   Postal Code

Telephone   (Res.)   (Bus.)   Fax No.
Number(s):

3. Service will be:

☐ Mailed Out

☐ Picked Up - **Call Box No.** _____ *(if applicable)*

☐ Edmonton

☐ Calgary

4. Type of Payment:

☐ Cash   ☐ Cheque No. _____   Account No. _____

☐ Visa ⊔⊔⊔⊔-⊔⊔⊔⊔-⊔⊔⊔⊔-⊔⊔⊔   ☐ Mastercard ⊔⊔⊔⊔-⊔⊔⊔⊔-⊔⊔⊔⊔-⊔⊔⊔⊔

Authorization Number   Expiry Date   Signature of Cardholder

5. Type of Service: *(check* ☑ *one only)*

☐ Partnership   ☐ Annual Return   ☐ Incorporation   ☐ Discharge Receiver

☐ Limited Partnership   ☐ Dissolution/Liquidation   ☐ Name Change   ☐ Appointment of Receiver

☐ Trade Name   ☐ Discontinuance   ☐ English/French Equivalent   ☐ Registration

☐ Photocopies   ☐ Revival/Restoration   ☐ Articles of Amendment   ☐ Fax

☐ Diazo Copies   ☐ Amalgamation   ☐ Restated Articles   ☐ Tax (G.S.T.)

☐ Certified Copies   ☐ Continuation   ☐ Object or Bylaws Amendments   ☐ Other *(explain below)*

Special Instructions for any of the above services: _____

Signature   Print Name

REG 3019 (96/05) FORM 79

WHITE - AUDIT   **WHITE - FILE**   **GREEN - CORPORATE REGISTRY**   **PINK - CLIENT**

SAMPLE #26
ARTICLES OF AMENDMENT

IMPORTANT: PLEASE READ INSTRUCTIONS ON THE BACK OF THIS FORM

BUSINESS CORPORATIONS ACT
(SECTION 27 OR 171)

FORM 4

Alberta
CONSUMER AND
CORPORATE AFFAIRS

ARTICLES OF AMENDMENT

1. NAME OF CORPORATION:	2. CORPORATE ACCESS NUMBER:
SKYWALK RESTAURANT LTD.	12345678

3. ITEM NO. _____1._____ OF THE ARTICLES OF THE ABOVE NAMED CORPORATION ARE AMENDED IN ACCORDANCE WITH

SECTION ___167(1)(a)___ OF THE BUSINESS CORPORATIONS ACT.

a) Name change to Highrise Restaurants Ltd.
   (Consent of High Ways Restaurants Ltd. is attached.)
   (Name approval is also attached.)

DATE	SIGNATURE	TITLE
June 1, 199-	*Stew Cooke*	President

FOR DEPARTMENTAL USE ONLY	FILED
CCA-06 104	

90

CONSENT AND UNDERTAKING

HIGH WAYS RESTAURANTS LTD. hereby consents to use of the name HIGHRISE RESTAU-RANTS LTD., and undertakes to either change its name or dissolve within six (6) months after the incorporation of the new Company.

In witness whereof HIGH WAYS RESTAURANTS LTD., has hereunto affixed its corporate seal under the hand of its duly authorized officers.

DATED at the City of Calgary, in the Province of Alberta, this 28th day of May, 199-.

HIGH WAYS RESTAURANTS LTD.

Per: _J. M. Smith_____
President and Director

RESOLUTION OF THE SHAREHOLDERS OF HIGHRISE RESTAURANTS LTD. PASSED EFFECTIVE AS OF THE 1ST DAY OF JUNE, 199-.

WHEREAS the Company wishes to increase its current number of directors from the present one (1) to two (2);

NOW THEREFORE BE IT UNANIMOUSLY RESOLVED that Carmel Cooke be appointed as director of the company effective as of the date hereof and that the Secretary of the Company be and is hereby authorized to do all such things as may be necessary to give effect to this change.

Stew Cooke
STEW COOKE

I, Carmel Cooke being the Secretary of Highrise Restaurants Ltd. do hereby certificate the foregoing to be a true and accurate copy of a Special Resolution of the Shareholders of the Company passed effective the 1st day of June, 199-, and that the same is in full force and effect unamended.

Carmel Cooke
CARMEL COOKE

SAMPLE #29
NOTICE OF CHANGE OF DIRECTORS

IMPORTANT: PLEASE READ INSTRUCTIONS ON THE BACK OF THIS FORM

BUSINESS CORPORATIONS ACT
(SECTIONS 101, 108 AND 276)

FORM 6

Alberta
CONSUMER AND
CORPORATE AFFAIRS

NOTICE OF DIRECTORS OR
NOTICE OF CHANGE OF DIRECTORS

1. NAME OF CORPORATION:	2. ALBERTA CORPORATE ACCESS NUMBER:
HIGHRISE RESTAURANTS LTD.	12345678

3. ON THE __1st__ DAY OF __June__ ,19 _9-_ , THE FOLLOWING PERSON(S) WERE **APPOINTED** DIRECTOR(S):

NAME	MAILING ADDRESS (INCLUDING **POSTAL CODE**)	RESIDENT CANADIAN?
Carmel Cooke	112 Eat Hardy Drive S.W. Calgary, Alberta Z1P 0G0	YES ☐ NO ☐
		YES ☐ NO ☐
		YES ☐ NO ☐

4. ON THE _____ DAY OF_____ , 19_____ , THE FOLLOWING PERSON(S) **CEASED** TO HOLD OFFICE AS DIRECTOR(S):

NAME	MAILING ADDRESS (INCLUDING **POSTAL CODE**)

5. AS OF THIS DATE, THE DIRECTOR(S) OF THE CORPORATION ARE:

NAME	MAILING ADDRESS (INCLUDING **POSTAL CODE**)	RESIDENT CANADIAN?
Stew Cooke	112 Eat Hardy Drive S.W. Calgary, Alberta Z1P 0G0	YES ☒ NO ☐
Carmel Cooke	112 Eat Hardy Drive S.W. Calgary, Alberta Z1P 0G0	YES ☒ NO ☐
		YES ☐ NO ☐
		YES ☐ NO ☐

6. TO BE COMPLETED ONLY BY ALBERTA CORPORATIONS:
   ARE AT LEAST HALF OF THE MEMBERS OF THE BOARD OF DIRECTORS RESIDENT CANADIANS ?

YES ☒   NO ☐

7. DATE:	SIGNATURE	TITLE
199- 06 02 YEAR MONTH DAY	Stew Cooke	President
		TELEPHONE NUMBER 297-1234
FOR DEPARTMENTAL USE ONLY		FILED ®

CCA-06.106

SAMPLE #30
SPECIAL RESOLUTION CHANGING ADDRESS

RESOLUTION OF THE BOARD OF DIREC-
TORS OF HIGHRISE RESTAURANTS LTD.
PASSED EFFECTIVE THE 1ST DAY OF
SEPTEMBER, 199- PURSUANT TO
CLAUSE 5.10 OF THE BY-LAWS OF THE
COMPANY.

RESOLVED that the registered office of the Company be changed to 9735 Wealthy Drive S.W., Calgary, Alberta Z1P 0G0.

Stew Cooke
STEW COOKE

Carmel Cooke
CARMEL COOKE

I, Carmel Cooke, being the Secretary of Highrise Restaurants Ltd. do hereby certificate the foregoing to be a true and accurate copy of a Special Resolution of the Shareholders of the Company passed effective the 1st day of September, 199-, pursuant to Clause 5.10 of the by-laws of the Company, and that the same is in full force and effect unamended.

DATED this 1st day of September, 199-.

Carmel Cooke
Carmel Cooke — Secretary

SAMPLE #31
NOTICE OF CHANGE OF ADDRESS

IMPORTANT: PLEASE READ INSTRUCTIONS ON THE BACK OF THIS FORM

BUSINESS CORPORATIONS ACT
(SECTION 19)

FORM 3

Alberta
CONSUMER AND
CORPORATE AFFAIRS

NOTICE OF ADDRESS OR
NOTICE OF CHANGE OF ADDRESS

1. NAME OF CORPORATION:	2. CORPORATE ACCESS NUMBER:
HIGHRISE RESTAURANTS LTD.	12345678

3. ADDRESS OF REGISTERED OFFICE (ONLY A STREET ADDRESS, INCLUDING POSTAL CODE, OR LEGAL LAND DESCRIPTION).

9735 Wealthy Avenue S.W., Calgary, Alberta Z1P 0G0

4. RECORDS ADDRESS (ONLY A STREET ADDRESS, INCLUDING POSTAL CODE, OR LEGAL LAND DESCRIPTION)

N/A

5. ADDRESS FOR SERVICE BY MAIL, IF DIFFERENT FROM ITEM 3 (ONLY A POST OFFICE BOX, INCLUDING POSTAL CODE).

N/A

6. DATE	SIGNATURE	TITLE
September 1, 199-	*Stew Cooke*	President
		TELEPHONE NO.
		297-1234
FOR DEPARTMENTAL USE ONLY		FILED

CCA-06 103

95

RESOLUTION OF THE BOARD OF DIRECTORS OF HIGHRISE RESTAURANTS LTD. PASSED EFFECTIVE THE 30TH DAY OF SEPTEMBER, 199- PURSUANT TO CLAUSE _____ OF THE COMPANY BY-LAWS

DIVIDEND

UPON MOTION IT WAS UNANIMOUSLY RESOLVED that the Company elect to pay a dividend in the amount of $10.00 per share on the outstanding Class E shares of the capital stock of the Company, such dividend to be payable forthwith.

Stew Cooke
Stew Cooke

Carmel Cooke
Carmel Cooke

4. Sale and transfer of shares

From time to time, shareholders in a company may want to sell their shares to other shareholders or third parties. Or the company may want to issue new shares out of the treasury to existing shareholders or potential investors.

The sale of shares by a shareholder is basically a private transaction between that shareholder and the prospective purchaser. The company itself is not involved except to the extent that it has an obligation to issue new share certificates and approve the transfer of shares. However, because all non-distributing companies have some restrictions on the transfer of shares, shares cannot be freely conveyed from a shareholder to a purchaser unless those share restrictions are met.

The share restriction in Highrise Restaurants Ltd. by-laws is that no shares can be transferred without the consent of the board of directors. Any of the shareholders of Highrise who wish to sell or transfer their shares must bring the matter before a meeting of the board of directors to obtain the board's approval. This would not be particularly onerous in a corporation of this type because a share transfer would probably not happen without all parties agreeing to the transfer. However, these formalities must be met or the share transfer cannot occur.

In the case of Highrise Restaurants Ltd., Mr. Cooke has decided to bring Mr. Hardy into the active operation of the company and has agreed to sell him 25 of his Class A voting shares. Sample #33 shows the necessary directors' minutes of the approval of the board of directors for this share transfer.

It is also a good idea to have a formal purchase share agreement between the purchaser and the seller of the shares like the one in Sample #34 between Mr. Cooke and Mr. Hardy. Once the directors have approved the share transfer, changes will have to be made in the following parts of the minute book:

(a) The shareholders' ledger will have to be changed to include Mr. Hardy as a Class A shareholder.

(b) The securities register will have to be updated to show the transfer of shares from Cooke to Hardy. (See Sample #35).

(c) The shareholders' ledger will have to be updated to include a page showing Hardy as a Class A shareholder. (See Sample #36.)

(d) A new certificate will have to be prepared in the name of Mr. Hardy for the Class A shares (with the necessary share restrictions on the share certificate) and Mr. Cooke's share certificates will also have to be altered so that he will now only have 75 Class A shares in the company.

When you transfer shares, sign the back of your old share certificate. This is known as "signing off" the share certificate. This converts the share certificate into "street form," which means that, subject to the restriction on the transfer of shares, the share is freely negotiable, like a dollar bill. To ensure that this certificate does not fall into unwanted hands, keep it in the minute book and write the word "cancelled" across it in bold letters. (See Sample #37.)

The transfer of shares from one shareholder to a third party does not increase the issued capital of the company. It is a private transaction between the two parties and creates some tax consequences between those parties. If Mr. Cooke makes money on the sale of his shares, he incurs a capital gain and is subject to personal tax on that gain. No corporate tax consequences are involved.

The other method of getting shares into the hands of a new shareholder is to have those shares issued from the authorized capital of the company, i.e., from the company treasury. This way, the existing shareholders do not give up any of their shares and there are no personal tax consequences involved. Issuing new shares affects the value of their shares, however, depending on how much is paid for the new shares.

Referring back to the formula in chapter 2, if the amount of the retained earnings is increased and the ratio of the retained earnings to shares remains the same, then the share prices for existing shareholders will remain the same. For example, assume that before any new shares are issued, the company had 100 issued shares and a retained earnings of $1 000 or a value of $10 per share. If the company issues another 100 shares for $500 only, it effectively reduces all of the shares in the company to a value of $7.50 per share.

There may be other considerations involved. If you want to entice a person to come into the company or put some money up, you may have to give that person a benefit at the expense of the existing shareholders.

Shares are issued from treasury pursuant to a directors' resolution. Sample #38 shows a resolution for Highrise Restaurants Ltd. giving Mr. Cooke an additional 100 Class A shares at $5 per share. The corporate minute book will have to be updated by issuing new share certificates for Mr. Cooke. As well, the shareholders' ledger and securities register will have to be updated.

There are no filing requirements with the Registrar of Companies for either a transfer of shares from one party to another or the issuance of new shares. However, these changes should be reflected in the annual corporate summary discussed later.

DIRECTORS' MINUTES FOR SHARE TRANSFER

MINUTES OF A MEETING OF THE DIRECTORS OF HIGHRISE RESTAURANTS LTD., HELD AT 9735 WEALTHY AVENUE S.W., CALGARY, ALBERTA, ON THE 31ST DAY OF OCTOBER, 199-, AT THE HOUR OF 11:00 O'CLOCK IN THE FORENOON.

PRESENT:

STEW COOKE

CARMEL COOKE

being the Directors of the Company.

Stew Cooke as Chairman of the Meeting and Carmel Cooke as Secretary thereof.

The Directors being present and having waived notice of the calling of the Meeting, the Meeting was declared to be regularly constituted.

TRANSFER OF SHARES:

The Chairman stated that Stew Cooke has requested the approval of the Board of Directors to the transfer of Twenty Five (25) Class A shares of the share capital of the Company from himself to E.T. Hardy.

UPON MOTION IT WAS UNANIMOUSLY RESOLVED THAT:

(1) the following transfers of share in the share capital of the Company be and are hereby approved:

TRANSFEROR	TRANSFEREE	NUMBER & CLASS OF SHARES
Stew Cooke	E.T. Hardy	25 Class A

(2) the Secretary be and is hereby authorized to cancel share certificate #1 for twenty-five (25) Class A shares presently registered in the name of Stew Cooke and to issue share certificate #3 in the name of E.T. Hardy, for twenty-five (25) fully paid and non-assessable Class A shares.

There being no further business, the Meeting, ON MOTION, terminated.

APPROVED: _Stew Cooke_
Chairman

I, being the Director of the above-named Company, consent hereby to the holding of this Meeting at the above time and place and I do hereby waive notice of this Meeting and of any irregularities or informalities in the holding thereof and do hereby ratify, acquiesce in and confirm the business transacted by the said Meeting.

Stew Cooke
Stew Cooke

SAMPLE #34
AGREEMENT TO PURCHASE SHARES

THIS AGREEMENT DATED this 1st day of May, A.D. 199- and effective as at the 1st day of April, 199-.

BETWEEN:

> E.T. HARDY, of the Northwest Territories, (hereinafter referred to as the "Purchaser"), OF THE FIRST PART

> — and —

> STEW COOKE, of the City of Calgary, in the Province of Alberta, (hereinafter referred to as the "Vendor"), OF THE SECOND PART

> — and —

> HIGHRISE RESTAURANTS LTD., a body corporate, duly registered to carry on business in the Province of Alberta, (hereinafter referred to as the "Company"), OF THE THIRD PART.

WHEREAS the Vendor currently is the owner of all the issued voting shares of the Company;

AND WHEREAS the Vendor is desirous of selling and conveying to the Purchaser a portion of his shares in the Company and the Purchaser is desirous of acquiring said shares pursuant to the terms and conditions of this agreement;

NOW WITNESSETH THAT in consideration of the sum of One ($1.00) Dollar per share plus all other good and valuable consideration the parties hereto agree as follows:

1.   The Vendor agrees to sell to the Purchaser or the Purchaser's nominee and the Purchaser or his nominee agrees to purchase from the Vendors 25% of the issued and outstanding Class "A" shares of the Company at and for the purchase price of One ($1.00) Dollar per share.

2.   The purchase price for the aforedescribed shares shall be paid by the Purchaser to the Vendors upon execution of this agreement by the Purchaser.

3.   The Vendor acknowledges that he has obtained the necessary consent and approval from the Board of Directors of the Company for the aforedescribed transfer of shares and annexed hereto and marked as Schedule "A" to this agreement is a true copy of the Resolution of the Board of Directors of the Company approving the share transfer to the Purchaser; the Vendor warrants that the shares are free and clear of all liens, charges, claims, and encumbrances and have been issued as fully paid and non-assessable.

4.   The Company hereby agrees to instruct its corporate secretary and solicitor to do the following:

   (a)   cancel the existing share certificates in the name of the Vendor;

   (b)   issue a new share certificate in favor of the Purchaser for all shares acquired pursuant to this agreement;

   (c)   make all necessary changes to the corporate minute book registries dealing with shareholders;

   (d)   submit all filings, if necessary or required; with the Alberta Companies Branch.

5.   The Vendor further acknowledges that he has caused the Board of Directors of the Company to appoint the Purchaser as a Director and annexed hereto as Schedule "B" is a copy of said appointment resolution.

6.   The Company hereby acknowledges said appointment and undertakes to instruct its corporate secretary and solicitor to:

   (a)   make all necessary changes to the Directors' Register in the corporate minute book;

   (b)   make all necessary filing with the Alberta Companies Branch to evidence the change of Directors.

7.   The parties agree to enter into and execute such further and other documents as may be necessary to give full and complete effect to this agreement and the terms herein expressed.

8.   This agreement shall enure to and be binding upon the heirs, executors, administrators and assigns of the parties hereto.

9.   The parties agree that for purposes of this agreement the effective date of this agreement shall be the 1st day of June, 199-.

     IN WITNESS WHEREOF the parties have hereunto set their hands and seals on the day and year first above written.

J. M. Witness
Witness

Stew Cooke
Stew Cooke

Q.C. Ewe
Witness

E. T. Hardy
E.T. Hardy

Per: _Stew Cooke_
Highrise Restaurants

PARTICULARS OF SHARE TRANSFERS OF ___ SKYWALK RESTAURANT LTD. – former name
HIGHRISE RESTAURANTS LTD. – new name

We, the undersigned owners and holders of shares of the above company, for value received, do hereby, by our respective attorneys (or personally as the case may be), duly appointed, respectively transfer and assign such shares as in the manner hereunder set forth:

NO. OF TRANSFER	DATE	COMMON OR PREFERENCE	CERTIFICATE SURRENDERED NUMBER	CERTIFICATE SURRENDERED SHARES	NAME OF TRANSFEROR	NAME OF TRANSFEREE	ADDRESS	CERTIFICATE ISSUED NUMBER	CERTIFICATE ISSUED SHARES	SIGNATURE OF TRANSFEROR OR ATTORNEY
1	May 1/9-	C			Treasury	Stew Cooke	112 Eat Hardy DR. SW, Calgary Z1P 0G0	1A	100	
2	May 1/9-	C			Treasury	Carmel Cooke	112 Eat Hardy Dr. SW, Calgary Z1P 0G0	1B	100	
3	May 1/9-	P			Treasury	E.T. Hardy	690 Tubby Avenue Calgary, Alberta Z1P 0G0	1C	50	
4	Oct 31/9-	C	1A	25	Stew Cooke	E.T. Hardy	as above	2A	25	
					Stew Cooke	Stew Cooke	112 Eat Hardy Dr. SW, Calgary Z1P 0G0	3A	75	

SAMPLE #36
UPDATED SHAREHOLDERS' LEDGER

NAME   STEW COOKE

ADDRESS   112 Eat Hardy Drive S.W.

           Calgary, Alberta Z1P OG0

OCCUPATION   Restauranteur

CLASS AND NOMINAL AMOUNT   CLASS A COMMON VOTING NPV
OF SHARES

DATE	No. OF CERTIFICATE ISSUED	No. OF CERTIFICATE CANCELLED	TRANSFER No.	TO OR FROM WHOM	FOLIO	PAID UP	SOLD SHARES	BOUGHT SHARES	BALANCE
May 1/9-	1A		1	From Treasury		$100		100	100
Oct 31/9-	2A & 3A	1A	4	To E.T. Harty and To Stew Cooke			25		75

103

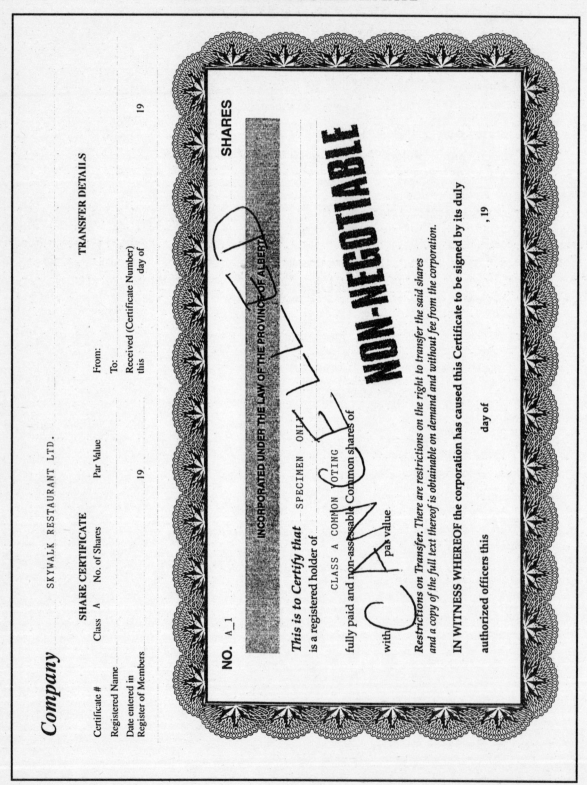

The undersigned, for valuable consideration received, hereby transfers to

Joe Smith
_____
(transferee)

100 Class A
_____
(number and class)

share(s) in the authorized capital of the within Company to hold unto the transferee, his heirs, executors, administrators and assigns, subject to the same conditions on which the transferor held at the time of execution, and the transferee in taking delivery hereof takes the said shares subject to the conditions aforesaid.

DATE June 15, 199—

SIGNATURE Stew Cooke

WITNESS J. M. Witness

RESOLUTION OF THE BOARD OF DIRECTORS OF HIGHRISE RESTAURANTS LTD. PASSED EFFECTIVE THE 2ND DAY OF NOVEMBER, 199- PURSUANT TO CLAUSE 5.10 OF THE BY-LAWS OF THE COMPANY.

WHEREAS Stew Cooke is desirous of subscribing for an additional one hundred (100) Class A shares in the capital stock of the Company.

NOW THEREFORE BE IT RESOLVED THAT:

The subscription of Stew Cooke for an additional one hundred (100) Class A shares in the capital stock of the Company be and is hereby approved;

The Secretary of the Company be and is hereby authorized to issue share certificate #4A for one hundred (100) Class A shares in the capital stock of the Company as fully paid and non-assessable for a price of $5.00 per share, and that the Company add to its stated capital account for the Class A shares the sum of $500.00.

_____
Stew Cooke

_____
Carmel Cooke

I, Carmel Cooke, being the Secretary of Highrise Restaurants Ltd. do hereby certificate the foregoing to be a true and accurate copy of a Special Resolution of the Shareholders of the Company passed effective the 2nd day of November, 199-, pursuant to Clause 5.10 of the by-laws of the Company, and that the same is in full force and effect unamended.

DATED this 2nd day of November, 199-

_____
Carmel Cooke — Secretary

5. Redemption or buying back of shares

The Business Corporations Act provides the mechanism for a company, under certain circumstances, to redeem or buy back its shares. The company must be able to meet the solvency requirements discussed earlier. Share redemption is done by resolution of the board of directors. There are tax consequences that could trigger a fundamental change. Never do this without professional advice. Although a company can redeem shares, those shares must be returned to the treasury. A company cannot hold shares in itself.

This contrasts with "retractable" shares. A shareholder has the right to sell retractable shares back to the company at a specific price at any time. A redeemable share can be purchased only at certain times.

6. Options and other employee benefits

If your business grows to the point where you are hiring employees, you may wish to consider instituting one of a number of programs or plans that are available to benefit employees. These may include the granting of share options, profit sharing plans, staff benefits, and discount plans.

It is very important to realize that the benefits of instituting one or more of the following plans works both ways: it obviously benefits your staff, but, at the same time, you will find that it will benefit the company. By maintaining a happy staff, productivity and morale will be high. Your staff will feel a real part of the operation and will no doubt provide invaluable assistance and dedication to the enterprise.

(a) Share options

A corporation, through its board, can grant to its employees the right to purchase its shares (either voting, non-voting, or preferred) for a set price over a predetermined period of time. Usually, the option price is less than the actual value of the share and,

therefore, acts as an incentive to employees to acquire an interest in the business at a discount.

(b) Profit-sharing plans

There are an infinite number of methods that you can devise that allow sharing of revenue or profit among some or all of your employees. Some of these plans, such as the Deferred Profit-Sharing Plan (DPSP) may provide significant tax benefits to the corporation.

(c) Staff benefit and discount plans

It may be an advantage to you, depending on the type of business you are in, to provide special bonuses or discounts to staff for the purchase of products or services available from the business. Alternatively, you may be able to arrange staff purchase discounts with other businesses that you deal with, such as your suppliers, tradespeople, customers, and consultants.

7. Special resolutions

There are two basic types of resolutions that shareholders or directors of a company can pass: special resolutions and ordinary resolutions.

An ordinary resolution requires a simple majority while a special resolution requires at least a two-thirds majority or a higher majority if the Articles provide for it. In the Articles of Incorporation for Highrise Restaurants Ltd., the majority requirement was increased to a 75% majority rather than a 66% majority. This effectively still gives Mr. Cooke control even though he has given up 25% of the voting shares to Mr. Hardy.

Special resolutions are required in cases where the company is making an extraordinary decision about one matter or another. Normally, the by-laws of the company or the unanimous shareholders' agreement determines whether or not an ordinary or a special resolution is required.

However, a good rule of thumb is that in situations dealing with major items, such as the removal of a director or the sale of all or most of the assets of the company, a special resolution is required.

If the company is governed by a unanimous shareholder agreement, it tells the company how its activities are governed, and a resolution may not be required.

As long as the resolution is set out and "certified true" by the corporate secretary or president, it is usually only necessary to reproduce the resolution that was passed rather than going to the time and trouble of drawing up a full set of corporate minutes. These certifications are accepted by most lenders as long as they are properly written and sealed.

8. Changes to Articles of Incorporation

As discussed earlier, the Articles of Incorporation may be amended by a special resolution of the shareholders. Any of the items in the Articles of Incorporation can be changed. These changes could include the creation of new classes of shares in item 2, the addition of share transfer restrictions in item 3, or changes to any of the provisions in item 6. Articles of Amendment have to be submitted to the Companies Branch and a copy filed in the minute book.

Many changes to the Articles of Incorporation are fundamental to the company because they are really changes to the rules under which the company is governed. This has been recognized in the Business Corporations Act, which deems that some of these changes are so fundamental in nature that they give special rights to shareholders who disagree with the changes. Those remedies will be discussed in chapter 6.

9. Changes to by-laws

Unlike the Articles of Incorporation, the by-laws of a company are internal documents and, therefore, can be amended without filing anything with the Companies Branch. The by-laws normally direct how a by-law is amended, but the act does provide that if there is no provision made for how by-laws are to be amended, it must be done in a two-step process.

The directors, by resolution, first propose the amendment; the amendment is then submitted to the shareholders who may by ordinary resolution confirm, reject, or amend the by-law. The amendment is effective from the date of the resolution of the directors until it is confirmed by the shareholders. If it is rejected by the shareholders, it then ceases to be effective.

In addition, a shareholder entitled to vote at an annual meeting may make a proposal to make, amend, or repeal a by-law in a shareholders' resolution. See section 131 of the Business Corporations Act for the details on how this can be done.

Sample #39 is a directors' resolution and a subsequent confirmation by the shareholders amending the by-laws of Highrise Restaurants Ltd. to change the director qualification requirements. Originally the company was set up so that directors did not have to own shares in the company to properly serve as a director. The changes require that any parties now or in the future who become directors of the company must own at least one voting share in the company in order to be properly qualified.

10. Registration of mortgages or debentures

From time to time in the course of its business, a company borrows money on the security of the assets that it owns. Often the security involved is that of a mortgage or a corporate debenture.

Under the Business Corporations Act, a corporate debenture or mortgage security is defined as a floating charge of a company's undertaking or property, or a charge on the goodwill of that company.

This security must be registered with the Personal Property Security Registry.

If there are two or more lenders, priority between lenders is normally established from the date of registration and not from the date documents are signed.

These types of security documents, although referred to as mortgages, do not include land mortgages, which are registered at the Land Titles Office. Therefore, if the company is giving a land mortgage only as security, it is not necessary to register that mortgage at the Personal Property Security Registry, but only at the Land Titles Office. Any other type of corporate debenture which secures property other than land, however, should be registered at the Personal Property Security Registry. For the location of a document registry nearest you, telephone 427-5104 in Edmonton.

In addition to the registration requirements, every company is required to keep at its records office or its registered office a copy of the document creating the registered mortgage or debenture (often known as the General Security Agreement), and a register of mortgages giving a short description of the property mortgaged, the amount of the mortgage, and the names of the mortgagees. This register must be open for inspection by any creditor or security holder for at least two business hours in each day and, if required, the corporation must provide copies of the register to creditors.

In order for it to be able to expand, Highrise Restaurants Ltd. has taken a loan from the Federal Business Development Bank in the amount of $50 000. That loan is secured on the assets of the restaurant in a General Security Agreement. The General Security Agreement is registered at the Personal Property Security Registry and will provide a floating charge over all the assets of the company.

A sample of the mortgage register that the company must maintain in its minute book as evidence of the registration of the General Security Agreement is shown in Sample #40.

RESOLUTION OF THE BOARD OF DIREC-
TORS OF HIGHRISE RESTAURANT LTD.
PASSED NOVEMBER 15TH, 199- EFFEC-
TIVE THE 15TH DAY OF NOVEMBER, 199-

UNANIMOUSLY RESOLVED as a Special Resolution of the Directors of Highrise Restaurants Ltd. that:

(a) The By-Laws of the Company be amended as follows:

(i) Article 4.04 be amended to read as follows:

No person shall be qualified for election as a director if he is less than 18 years of age; if he is
of unsound mind and has been so found by a court in Canada or elsewhere; if he is not an
individual; or if he has the status of a bankrupt. A director must hold at least one Class A share
in the Company in order to be a properly qualified director.

DATED at the City of Calgary, in the Province of Alberta, this 15th day of November, 199-.

Stew Cooke
Stew Cooke

Carmel Cooke
Carmel Cooke

Certified a true copy of a resolution of the Board of Directors of Highrise Restaurants Ltd.,
the 15th day of November, 199-.

Carmel Cooke
Secretary

RESOLUTION OF THE SHAREHOLDERS
OF HIGHRISE RESTAURANTS LTD.
PASSED NOVEMBER 17TH, 199- EFFEC-
TIVE THE 17TH DAY OF NOVEMBER, 199-

RESOLVED as an Ordinary Resolution of the Shareholders of Highrise Restaurants Ltd. that:

1. The amendment to article 4.04 of the By-laws of the Company proposed by the Directors of the Company by way of Special Resolution dated November 15, 199- be and is hereby ratified;

2. The Corporate Secretary is instructed to make all necessary changes to the By-laws and undertake any further matters that may be required.

DATED at the City of Calgary, in the Province of Alberta, this 17th day of November, 199-.

_____
Stew Cooke

_____
E.T. Hardy

being all the voting shareholders of the Company.

Certified a true copy of this 17th day of November, 199-

_____
Secretary

SAMPLE #40
MORTGAGE REGISTER

REGISTER OF MORTGAGES OF _____ HIGHRISE RESTAURANTS LTD. _____

DATE OF MORTGAGE	TYPE OF MORTGAGE	SHORT DESCRIPTION OF PROPTERY MORTGAGED	AMOUNT OF MORTGAGE	NAME OF MORTGAGEE OR PERSONS ENTITLED TO MORTGAGE	WHERE AND WHEN REGISTERED OR FILED	DATE OF SATISFACTION DISCHARGE OR CANCELLATION
Dec 1/9-	General Security Agreement	floating charge on assets of restaurant	$50,000.00	Federal Business Development Bank	Cos. Br. -Dec 8/9- Central Reg. - Dec 10/9-	

6
OBLIGATIONS OF INCORPORATION

a. ANNUAL REQUIREMENTS

A company does have some ongoing annual obligations that it is required to meet in order to keep in good standing. Basically these requirements include holding an annual general meeting and filing an annual corporate summary.

1. Annual general meeting

Every company is required by law to hold an annual meeting of shareholders. The first meeting must be held not later than 18 months after the date of incorporation. At that meeting, the shareholders are entitled to attend not only to discuss certain specific business but to question the directors about general corporate matters. The main purposes for the annual meeting are as follows:

(a) Election and/or confirmation of directors and officers

(b) Ratification of directors' conduct of past business affairs

(c) Appointment of auditors if required

(d) Presentation of financial report

(e) Discussion between the shareholders and the board about the past performance of the company and prospects for the upcoming year

The by-laws state the notice requirements for the meeting and where the meeting is to be held. The meeting can be held by telephone if all shareholders can be in contact with each other at all times. In fact, no meeting at all is necessary if the shareholders are prepared to waive notice of the meeting and sign the minutes as prepared.

In most small non-distributing corporations, the annual shareholders' meeting is only a formality. However, it does offer a good opportunity for all those involved in the affairs of the company to reflect on the past year's operations and to make some projections as to the company's business in the forthcoming year.

As well, any minority shareholders who have complaints or wish to make suggestions about how the business should be run can use the annual general meeting as an opportunity to voice their opinions.

The minutes of the annual general meeting of Highrise Restaurants Ltd. are shown in Samples #41 and #42. One set is by the shareholders and the other by the directors. They basically repeat the items listed above. The company has decided not to appoint an auditor for the next year and has approved all of the acts of the directors that had taken place during the last year. The same directors were re-elected. These minutes are very basic and can be used by most companies each year.

Shareholders entitled to vote at an annual meeting may also submit proposals. Under the law, the corporation has a certain obligation to circulate these proposals to all the other shareholders. Again, see section 131 of the Business Corporations Act for details.

A shareholder who cannot personally attend a meeting and who is entitled to vote may register that vote by giving a proxy to a shareholder or other party who will be attending the meeting. In effect, the proxy is a limited power of attorney giving the individual who holds the proxy the right to vote the absentee shareholder's shares as directed by that shareholder.

There will be few occasions when a proxy is required in a small non-distributing company, but there are situations where, if a crucial vote is taken, a proxy would be worthwhile. There is no special form required for a proxy; it can be very informal, but it must be in writing.

In addition to the annual shareholders' meeting, special meetings of the shareholders can be called by the board of directors and, in some cases, by shareholders, in accordance with the by-laws of the company. At these special meetings, special business of the company, such as the sale of all or substantially all the assets of the company or a change of business direction for the company, can be discussed.

Full notice of the special meeting should be provided as well as information about what will be discussed at that meeting. Shareholders can waive the notice provisions in the same way they waived notice of the annual meeting.

2. Annual Return

Once your company is in operation, except for filings required as a result of changes, the only regular filing that it has to make is the Annual Return (Form 22). At the time of writing, there is a $20 fee for filing this report.

Sample #43 shows an Annual Return for Highrise Restaurants Ltd. Note that the directors and shareholders of the company must be listed with full addresses and occupations. The registered office of the company must also be listed. If there are more than five shareholders, only the five shareholders with the largest holdings must be listed along with the different classes of shares they hold. A recent revision to the form requires the corporation to disclose if it is engaged in any activities that may result in receipt of revenue. Presumably, this is for provincial income tax collection purposes.

The Annual Return should be submitted to the Registrar by one of the officers of the company in the anniversary month of incorporation. For example, since Highrise Restaurants Ltd. was incorporated in August, its annual corporate summary has to be filed in the month of August.

Failure to file the Annual Return on time will result in your company being subject to dissolution by the Registrar. Normally, the Registrar will insert a warning on the form advising that the corporation will automatically be dissolved if all annual returns are not made current by a certain date. This could have serious consequences for the company and could ultimately lead to it losing its assets and being unable to carry on business.

Accordingly, it is always wise to mark your calendar with the month of incorporation so you can promptly file the Annual Return. It is easiest to do it in conjunction with the annual meeting so that both matters can be dealt with at the same time.

The Corporate Registry no longer sends you back a copy of the Annual Return marked "Filed." Instead you will receive a confirmation letter (see Sample #44). You should make a copy of the Annual Return before you send it in and place it in the Minute Book. When you receive the confirmation letter from the Corporate Registry, attach it to your copy of the Annual Return and file it on the minute book.

b. FUNDAMENTAL CHANGE

The concept of fundamental change is a relatively new one in Alberta law. It is primarily designed to provide minority shareholders with some specific remedies (i.e., ways of enforcing their rights). Although these remedies were designed to assist minority shareholders of larger companies, they also apply to small non-distributing companies. If you have any minority shareholders, you should be aware of the rights and remedies that minority shareholders now have.

HIGHRISE RESTAURANTS LTD.
                                  199-

COMPANY NAME   YEAR

Unanimous Annual Minutes of Shareholders

WHEREAS the Articles of the Company permit Resolution by unanimous consent of all Shareholders;

AND WHEREAS this Minute is a written Minute of a Resolution fully executed on a date other than the effective date;

AND WHEREAS the Business Corporations Act of the Province of Alberta requires that an Annual General Meeting be held;

AND WHEREAS it is expedient to hold the said Meeting by way of unanimous written Resolution circulated to all of the Shareholders;

Resolution

NOW THEREFORE the Shareholders of the Company unanimously resolve as follows:

1. THAT all acts, contracts, by-laws, proceedings, appointments, elections and payments enacted, made, done, taken and paid by the Directors and Officers of the Company since the date of the last annual general meeting or minutes and as set out or referred to in the Minutes and Resolutions of the Board of Directors of the Company be and the same are hereby approved, sanctioned and confirmed.

2. THAT the appointments and offices of the present Board of Directors be and the same are hereby confirmed and accordingly that all present members of the Board are hereby re-appointed to the Board for a further term of one year.

3. THAT the Company and the Shareholders thereof hereby waive and dispense with the necessity for an Annual General Meeting save as by unanimous consent to this round-robin Resolution.

4. THAT this Resolution shall be effective as at the date of the execution of the last Shareholder as below indicated.

5. THAT the Company do not have an audit performed on its accounts for the fiscal year most recently ended, and that an auditor for the Company not be appointed for the forthcoming year.

SAMPLE #41 — Continued

Unanimously executed on the dates below indicated by all of the Shareholders of Highrise Restaurants Ltd.

Executed this ___1st___)
day of ___April___ , 199-___)

Stew Cooke
Stew Cooke

Executed this ___1st___)
day of ___April___ , 199-___)

Carmel Cooke
Carmel Cooke

Executed this ___1st___)
day of ___April___ , 199-___)

E. T. Hardy
E. T. Hardy

Executed this _____)
day of _____ , 19___)

_____

SECRETARY'S CERTIFICATE

I, Secretary of the within Company hereby certify this to be a true extract from a unanimous written resolution of the Shareholders of the Company.

Carmel Cooke
Secretary   Carmel Cooke

HIGHRISE RESTAURANTS LTD.   199-_____

COMPANY NAME   YEAR

Unanimous Annual Minutes of Directors

WHEREAS the Articles of the Company permit Resolution by unanimous consent of all Directors;

AND WHEREAS this Minute is a written Minute of a Resolution fully executed on a date other than the effective date;

AND WHEREAS the Business Corporations Act of the Province of Alberta requires that an Annual General Meeting be held;

AND WHEREAS it is expedient to hold the said Meeting by way of unanimous written Resolution circulated to all of the Directors;

Resolution

NOW THEREFORE the Directors of the Company unanimously resolve as follows:

1. THAT all acts, contracts, by-laws, proceedings, appointments, elections and payments enacted, made, done, taken and paid by the Officers of the Company since the date of the last minutes of the Board of Directors of the Company be and the same are hereby approved, sanctioned and confirmed.

2. THAT the appointments of the Officers of the Company be and the same are hereby confirmed and accordingly that all present Officers of the Company are hereby re-appointed for a further term of one year.

3. THAT this Resolution shall be effective as at the date of the execution of the last Director as below indicated.

Unanimously executed on the dates below indicated by all of the Directors of
Highrise Restaurants Ltd.

Executed this ___1st___)
day of ___April___, 199-___)
        Stew Cooke
        Stew Cooke

Executed this ___1st___)
day of ___April___, 199-___)
        Carmel Cooke
        Carmel Cooke

Executed this ___1st___)
day of ___April___, 199-___)
        E. T. Hardy
        E. T. Hardy

Executed this _____)
day of _____; 199-___)

SECRETARY'S CERTIFICATE

I, Secretary of the within Company hereby certify this to be a true extract from a unanimous written resolution of the Directors of the Company.

        Carmel Cooke
Secretary   Carmel Cooke

SAMPLE #43
ANNUAL RETURN

Alberta

Business Corporations Act

ANNUAL RETURN

Consumer and Corporate Affairs Corporate Registry	8th Floor 10365 - 97 Street Edmonton, Alberta T5J 3W7 (403) 427-2311	3rd Floor, Canada Place 407 - 2nd Street S.W. Calgary, Alberta T2P 2Y3 (403) 297-3442

① CORPORATE ACCESS NO. ___12345678___

① FOR THE YEAR ENDING 19 _9-_____

② CORPORATION NAME

① DATE OF INCORPORATION, CONTINUANCE, AMALGAMATION

OR REGISTRATION: ___9- 04 17___
YY MM DD

HIGHRISE RESTAURANTS LTD.
③ ADDRESS

9735 Wealthy Drive S.W., Calgary, Alberta Z1P 0G0

④ HAS THERE BEEN A CHANGE OF DIRECTORS?   YES ☒ NO ☐
⑤ IF YES, HAS FORM 6 BEEN PREVIOUSLY   FILED ☒   or ATTACHED ☐
⑥ DOES THIS CORPORATION OWN CONTROLLED LAND   YES ☐ NO ☒
⑦ IS THE CORPORATION CURRENTLY ENGAGED IN ANY ACTIVITIES WHICH MAY RESULT IN RECEIPT OF REVENUE OF ANY KIND?   YES ☒ NO ☐

⑩ SHAREHOLDERS

% OF VOTING
SHARES ISSUED

NAME Stew Cooke

ADDRESS   9735 Wealthy Drive S.W.

Calgary, Alberta Z1P 0G0

CORPORATE ACCESS NUMBER ___12345678___   ___75___ %

NAME E.T. Hardy

ADDRESS   111 Uprising Road S.W.
Calgary, Alberta Z1P 0G0

CORPORATE ACCESS NUMBER ___12345678___   ___25___ %

NAME

ADDRESS

CORPORATE ACCESS NUMBER _____   ____ %

NAME

ADDRESS

CORPORATE ACCESS NUMBER _____   ____ %

NAME

ADDRESS

CORPORATE ACCESS NUMBER _____   ____ %

INSTRUCTIONS FOR COMPLETION OF THIS FORM ON REVERSE SIDE

⑪ DATE April 2, 199-	⑫ SIGNATURE *Stew Cooke*	⑬ TELEPHONE BUS. 297-1234 RES.	⑭ FILED (FOR DEPT. USE ONLY)

Corporate Registry

8th floor, John E.Brownlee Building
10365 - 97 Street
Edmonton, Alberta
Canada T5J 3W7

Telephone 403/427-2311
Fax 403/422-1091

September 6, 199-

HIGHRISE RESTAURANTS LTD.
9735 Wealthy Drive S.W.
Calgary, Alberta
Z1P 0G0

199- ANNUAL RETURN PROOF OF FILING

The 199- annual return for:

HIGHRISE RESTAURANTS LTD.
was filed on September 1, 199-.

Payment received: $20.00

This is the only confirmation you will receive.

The following items are defined in the act as fundamental changes:

(a) Change of name (other than a change from a numbered company name to a word name)

(b) Changes in the restriction on the business that the company can carry on

(c) Important changes in the capital structure and rights of shareholders

(d) Any other changes in the Articles of Incorporation

(e) Amalgamations and re-organizations

(f) Sales or lease of substantially all of the property of the company

If any of the above matters are dealt with, certain procedures must be followed by the board of directors, and in some cases, shareholders have more remedies than those available to them at common law.

The normal procedure involved in implementing a fundamental change is for the board of directors to enact a special resolution and submit it to the shareholders. When submitting it to the shareholders, the directors will have to give full notice to all of the shareholders and in those areas where the special remedies exist, provide shareholders with notice of those special remedies.

The two most important special remedies are the right of shareholders to vote on certain issues even if their shares are non-voting shares, and the right to be bought out of the company at the fair market value of their shares if they strongly disagree with proposed changes.

For example, if a company wants to sell or lease all or substantially all of its property, all shareholders have the right to vote, whether or not their shares normally carry the right to vote. As well, if those shareholders disagree with the decision by the company, they have the right to have the company buy their shares from them at fair market value.

These changes to the law are new to Alberta and provide significantly more protection for minority shareholders than they have in the past. It is necessary, therefore, for the company to ensure that those rights of the minority shareholders are properly dealt with and that shareholders receive all the notice that they are entitled to.

The following is a list of situations where shareholders have the right to dissent and be bought out of the company:

(a) Changes in any restrictions on the business which may be carried on by the company

(b) Changes in the capital structure of the company (if the changes in the capital structure affect in any way the shares of that particular class held by the shareholder)

(c) Constraints on share transfers (if it affects the class of shares held by the shareholder)

(d) An amalgamation of the company with another company

(e) Change of jurisdiction of the company from Alberta to another province

(f) Sale or lease of substantially all of the property of the company

The following is a list of fundamental changes on which all shareholders have the right to vote whether or not their shares are normally non-voting:

(a) Changes in capital structure as above

(b) Amalgamations

(c) Change of jurisdiction

(d) Sale or lease of substantially all the property of the company

In all other cases involving fundamental change, there are no buy-out rights or additional voting rights given to minority shareholders; however, proper notice must be given to all shareholders along with details of the changes that are being proposed.

If your company is faced with a decision that will qualify as a fundamental change, and you are the slightest bit unsure about what procedures to follow to properly put the changes into effect, I suggest that you obtain professional advice.

c. SHAREHOLDERS' REMEDIES

I have already noted the right of shareholders to be bought out of the company if they dissent on certain fundamental changes, as well as the right of shareholders to put forward a "proposal" at an annual shareholders' meeting.

In addition to those rights, you should be aware that shareholders have the right to maintain a lawsuit on behalf of the company even if the company itself is reluctant to begin the action. This action is known as a derivative action. The party that brings the action must be able to show that it appears to be in the interest of the company that the action be brought and maintained.

As well, a shareholder now has the right to apply to the court for an order to prevent the company from becoming involved in an activity which would be "oppressive or unfairly prejudicial to, or that unfairly disregards the interests of any shareholder, creditor, director, or officer of the company."

This is a very wide, general power and gives a substantial amount of discretion to the courts as to how they will deal with any particular problem. The court has the right to make any interim or final order that it thinks fit, including restraining orders, orders appointing receivers, or orders regulating the company's affairs by actually amending the Articles or by-laws, or even amending a unanimous shareholders' agreement.

In addition, a shareholder has the right to apply to the courts for an order dissolving a corporation if it has failed for two or more consecutive years to comply with the requirements for annual meetings, carried on business or exercised powers restricted by the Articles, failed to provide access to corporate records, or failed to permit the examination of statements or provide financial statements.

The court also has the power to order an investigation of a company if a shareholder applies to the court and can prove to the court that the business of the company has been carried on with the intent to defraud a person or that the oppressive or unfairly prejudicial manner of operation of the business has been such as to affect or disregard the interest of a shareholder.

Shareholders of companies should also be aware that they are deemed to be insiders of a company in connection with any share transaction if they make use of any specific confidential information for their own benefit or advantage, which affects materially the value of the share. They may have to compensate an injured party for losses and may also be accountable to the company for its losses if damages are incurred because of the use of this special information.

d. AMALGAMATION

For purposes of consolidation, tax considerations, cost cutting, or any one of a number of other business reasons, your company may wish to amalgamate with one or more other companies. The legal effect of an amalgamation is that two or more companies that existed prior to amalgamation will, upon amalgamation, cease to exist and a new company known as the amalgamated company will come into existence.

Because of the strict requirements set down by the Business Corporations Act in order to allow an amalgamation to proceed, as well as the tax implications involved, you should get professional assistance from both a lawyer and an accountant prior to amalgamating. You should also be aware that an amalgamation qualifies as a fundamental change under the Business Corporations Act, which gives all shareholders the right to vote on the amalgamation and all dissenting shareholders the right to be bought out.

e. DISSOLUTION AND REVIVAL

As discussed in chapter 2, a company has a continuing existence even though the shareholders of the company may come and go. In order to dissolve or "wind up" a company, some action either by the company itself, a shareholder, or the Registrar of Companies must be taken.

These actions are divided into voluntary and involuntary methods of dissolution. I will discuss them briefly, but if you are contemplating dissolving your company, you should obtain professional advice from your lawyer and accountant.

In many instances, the best way of letting a company die is simply not to make any further filings with the Companies Branch. After a certain number of missed years (usually two consecutive years), the company will be struck off the register, which means that it can no longer legally carry on business in the province of Alberta.

The company then exists in a state of limbo because although it has not been officially dissolved, it cannot carry on business. There is no liability attached to any of the directors or shareholders of the company for allowing the company to fall into this position as long as this is a decision made by all the shareholders and directors. This should be done in a unanimous joint resolution of the directors and shareholders, which basically would be the last act that the company takes. A copy of that type of resolution is shown in Sample #45. From that point forward, the company should not carry on any further business.

This method is not advised if the company has any assets whatsoever because those assets will be frozen and will be of no use either to the company or to the shareholders. To get the company out of this state of limbo, it must be revived. Revivals are discussed later.

1. Voluntary dissolution

A voluntary dissolution or liquidation by a company can be accomplished in a proposal as defined in section 131 of the Business Corporations Act.

The more common method is to dissolve by special resolution of the shareholders or, if the company has issued more than one class of shares, by special resolution of the holders of each class whether or not those shareholders are otherwise entitled to vote. Form 17 — Articles of Dissolution — must be filed with the Registrar of Companies (see Sample #46).

Once the Registrar issues a Certificate of Intent to Dissolve (see Sample #47), the company can no longer carry on business except to do what is necessary to complete the liquidation. The company has the responsibility of collecting its assets, disposing of its properties, paying its debts, and finally distributing the balance of the monies to its shareholders.

2. Involuntary dissolution

Involuntary dissolution means dissolution that is normally initiated by the Registrar of Companies. The Business Corporations Act provides that if a company has not begun business within three years after the date shown on its Certificate of Incorporation, has not carried on business for three consecutive years or is in default for one year in filing any notice or document required, the Registrar may dissolve the company by issuing a Certificate of Dissolution. The Registrar also has a second option of applying to the courts for an order dissolving the corporation.

These are harsh provisions and in all likelihood are only used by the Registrar in unusual circumstances. The Registrar would probably go for the court order only if the company did have some assets but the Registrar thought the company should be dissolved.

SPECIAL RESOLUTION OF THE DIRECTORS AND SHAREHOLDERS OF HIGH-RISE RESTAURANTS LTD. PASSED EFFECTIVE THE 3RD DAY OF MARCH, 199-, PURSUANT TO SECTION 204 OF THE BUSINESS CORPORATION ACT OF THE PROVINCE OF ALBERTA.

UPON MOTION IT WAS UNANIMOUSLY RESOLVED THAT:

1. The Company be wound up voluntarily in pursuance of the provisions of Section 204 of the BUSINESS CORPORATIONS ACT;

2. In addition to and not by way of limitation upon the powers otherwise possessed by the Company, the said Company be and is hereby authorized:

   (a) to sell or otherwise dispose of, in block or in parcels, the real and personal property, effects and things in action of the Company by public auction or private sale and for such consideration and on such terms and conditions as he may see fit;

   (b) to distribute the property and assets of the Company in kind, specie or otherwise, in accordance with the Plan of Liquidation attached hereto;

   (c) to postpone the distribution of any property and assets of the Company for such period of time as the Company may see fit with a view to selling or otherwise disposing of the same, such period, however, not to exceed three years from the date hereof unless extended by the Company in general meeting;

   (d) to otherwise act in accordance with the laws set down in the Business Corporations Act and amendments thereto.

Stew Cooke
_____
Stew Cooke

E.T. Hardy
_____
E.T. Hardy

SAMPLE #46
ARTICLES OF DISSOLUTION
(SECTIONS 203 AND 204)

IMPORTANT: PLEASE READ INSTRUCTIONS ON THE BACK OF THIS FORM

BUSINESS CORPORATIONS ACT
(SECTIONS 203 AND 204)

FORM 17

Alberta
CONSUMER AND
CORPORATE AFFAIRS

ARTICLES OF DISSOLUTION

1. NAME OF CORPORATION:	2. CORPORATE ACCESS NUMBER:
HIGHRISE RESTAURANTS LTD.	12345678

3. THE CORPORATION HAS:

(a) ☐ NOT ISSUED ANY SHARES, HAS NO PROPERTY AND NO LIABILITIES

(b) ☐ NO PROPERTY AND NO LIABILITIES

(c) ☐ LIABILITIES

(d) ☒ NOT SENT A STATEMENT OF REVOCATION OF INTENT TO DISSOLVE

4. DOCUMENTS AND RECORDS OF THE CORPORATION SHALL BE KEPT FOR SIX YEARS FROM THE DATE OF DISSOLUTION BY:

President

NAME: Stew Cooke

ADDRESS:

9735 Wealthy Drive, S.W., Calgary, Alberta Z1P 0G0

5. IF APPLICATION IS MADE UNDER SECTION 204 OF THE BUSINESS CORPORATIONS ACT, HAS THIS CORPORATION COMPLIED WITH SECTION 204(7) OF THE ACT.

YES ☒   NO ☐

6. DATE	SIGNATURE	TITLE
March 3, 199-	*Stew Cooke*	President
FOR DEPARTMENTAL USE ONLY		FILED

SAMPLE #47
CERTIFICATE OF INTENT TO DISSOLVE

BUSINESS CORPORATIONS ACT
FORM 20
CERTIFICATE OF INTENT TO DISSOLVE

HIGHRISE RESTAURANTS LTD.   12345678
Name of Corporation   Corporate Access No.

   I hereby certify that the above mentioned corporation intends to dissolve under Section 204 of the Business Corporations Act as set out in the attached Statement of Intent to Dissolve.

Registrar   Date of Intent to Dissolve

J. M. Registrar   April 7, 199-

If the Registrar goes to court, the company must be given 120 days' written notice in the *Alberta Gazette*. The company, of course, has the right to attend the court hearing and contest the application or rectify any deficiencies within the 120-day period.

As mentioned before, a shareholder has the right to apply to the court to wind up a company if that shareholder can show that the actions of the company are "unfairly prejudicial or oppressive" to his or her rights as a shareholder.

The court can also order that a company be dissolved if it is satisfied that it is "just and equitable" that the corporation be liquidated and dissolved. This "just and equitable" power is a carry-over from earlier law and gives the court wide discretion to examine a situation involving the shareholders and the company. However, the courts are loathe to dissolve a company if it would mean a loss of employment for individuals or if property rights would be affected.

Companies should, of course, be on guard to avoid falling into any of the traps that could lead the Registrar to use the involuntary dissolution procedure. In practice, the Registrar is not waiting for the mail each day with a calendar in one hand and a court application to dissolve in the other. However, the law is there, and you should be aware that it is available to the Registrar simply to ensure that corporate filing requirements are met each year.

3. Revival

What happens if the Registrar does dissolve your company or if a company has voluntarily agreed not to carry on business? Can your company ever operate again?

Even if a company has been dissolved by the Registrar, any person can apply to the Registrar to revive the company. Articles of Revival must be completed and submitted to the Registrar (see Sample #48) along with a $300 filing fee. In the Articles of Revival, the person who is applying must tell the Registrar the reasons for dissolution and the reasons the company seeks a revival.

Assuming that the application is complete and proper, the Registrar has no choice but to issue a Certificate of Revival.

The corporation will be deemed to have been revived on the date shown on that certificate.

Once revived, the company will be deemed not to have been dissolved at all, subject to any terms imposed by the Registrar to protect the rights and privileges of individuals who may have acquired rights after the involuntary dissolution.

For a company incorporated before February 1, 1982, which has been dissolved, a shareholder or director of that company can apply to the court for a revival order. Certain court documents have to be filed and other information obtained. Legal advice is recommended because not only will the company have to be revived, but it will also have to be continued under the Business Corporations Act. (See chapter 7.)

Similarly, an active company under the old Companies Act that is dissolved because it failed to apply for continuance under the Business Corporations Act within the three-year time limit can apply to the court for an order reviving the company. The court can make an order reviving the company under the terms and conditions that it sees fit to impose.

To revive a company incorporated under the Business Corporations Act, the procedure is simple and a court application is not always necessary. Any interested party can apply to the court to revive. It does not necessarily have to be a shareholder, but can be a creditor or officer of the company. This procedure may also be used when a company has voluntarily decided not to continue on in business, but has not gone the formal dissolution route. Once revived, the company will be deemed to have been carrying on business continually during the period it was inactive.

f. CONCLUSION

The information in this and previous chapters should be sufficient to allow you to incorporate and operate your company in the normal course of events for the foreseeable future. Any unusual or complex circumstances that may come up and are not covered in these chapters will probably require professional assistance.

The next chapter discusses how to register your company in another province. Chapters 8 and 9 discuss other considerations of carrying on business in Alberta including some tax advantages and licensing requirements.

SAMPLE #48
ARTICLES OF REVIVAL

BUSINESS CORPORATIONS ACT
(SECTION 201)

FORM 15

Alberta

CONSUMER AND
CORPORATE AFFAIRS

ARTICLES OF REVIVAL

1. NAME OF DISSOLVED CORPORATION.	2. CORPORATE ACCESS NO.
HIGHRISE RESTAURANTS LTD.	12345678

3. REASON FOR DISSOLUTION.

a) Decided to sell restaurant business and no further need for corporation

4. INTEREST OF APPLICANT IN REVIVAL OF CORPORATION.

a) President and majority shareholder

b) I am desirous of opening up another restaurant using this company

5. NAME OF APPLICANT.	6. ADDRESS OF APPLICANT.
Stew Cooke	9735 Wealthy Drive S.W. Calgary, Alberta Z1P 0G0

SIGNATURE OF APPLICANT	DATE
Stew Cooke	November 15, 199-

FOR DEPARTMENTAL USE ONLY	FILED
CCA-06.115	

127

7

HOW TO REGISTER YOUR COMPANY IN ANOTHER PROVINCE

a. EXTRA-PROVINCIAL REGISTRATION

Extra-provincial registration refers to registration of your company in another province so you can carry on business in that other province. For purposes of this chapter, I will use the phrase "foreign jurisdiction" to refer either to the provinces other than Alberta or to a "federal" jurisdiction.

Many times, a company begins business operations in one province but because of expansion or business opportunity decides to expand into another province. Instead of setting up a brand new company in that other province, the company usually wants to keep only one corporation with the head office in the home province.

In order to carry on business or borrow money in a foreign jurisdiction, you must register your company in the foreign jurisdiction. There are also occasions when for one reason or another, your company may wish to change jurisdictions and switch from being a company that is incorporated provincially in Alberta to a company that is incorporated federally or vice versa. Procedures for these types of changes, known as "continuations" are also provided for by both federal and provincial legislation.

This chapter covers the requirements for companies incorporated outside of Alberta to register in Alberta and for Alberta companies to register in a foreign jurisdiction. It also reviews the method of continuing an Alberta company as a foreign jurisdiction company and continuing a foreign jurisdiction company as an Alberta company.

b. REGISTERING FOREIGN JURISDICTION COMPANIES IN ALBERTA

1. Registration requirements

Extra-provincial companies are required to register in Alberta to provide residents and business people of this province with basic information about the company and with a place and a person where legal documents in Alberta may be properly served.

It is only when a company "carries on business" in Alberta that it is required to become registered in Alberta. Under the Business Corporations Act, a company is deemed to be carrying on business in Alberta if —

(a) its name or any name under which it carries on business is listed in a telephone directory for any part of Alberta or appears in any advertisement in which an address in Alberta is given,

(b) it has a resident agent or representative or a warehouse office, or place of business in Alberta,

(c) it solicits business in Alberta,

(d) it is the owner of any estate or interest in land in Alberta,

(e) it is licensed or registered or required to be licensed or registered under any act of Alberta entitling it to do business,

(f) it holds a motor vehicle certificate, or

(g) it otherwise carries on business in Alberta.

You can see by the above (which is from a section of the Business Corporations Act) that this covers just about every practical definition of carrying on business or business activity that may be found. Any company that falls within any of those definitions is required to register extra-provincially in Alberta.

A federal company has by definition the right to carry on business in Alberta without having to register. However, the province has jurisdiction to pass laws requiring it to be properly registered or licensed for administrative purposes. Accordingly, even a federal company may have to register extra-provincially in this province for certain things, even if the head office of that company is in Alberta.

(a) Application forms and documents

In order to register extra-provincially, the following documents must be submitted to the Registrar of Companies:

(a) Form 24 — Statement of Registration of Extra-Provincial Corporation

(b) Form 27 — Notice of Attorney for Service

(c) Certified copies of the incorporating documents and amendments

(d) Certificate of Status

For purposes of illustrating how the extra-provincial registration procedure works, assume that there is a British Columbia company known as West Coast Publishing Ltd. that wants to sell advertising in the province of Alberta. In order to do so it will need a sales office here and, accordingly, will have to register extra-provincially.

West Coast Publishing must complete the State of Registration for the Extra-Provincial Corporation, which requires information about the name, date of incorporation, place of incorporation, head office, and principal business of the corporation.

All the information required for the Statement of Registration should be readily available to you in your minute book. The registration form should be signed under seal by the signing officers for the company. See Sample #49 for the Statement of Registration filed by West Coast Publishing Ltd.

The Notice of Attorney for Service form appoints the legal representative of the company in this province. The address is necessary (a post office box is not sufficient) in order that legal documents can be served on the attorney at that address. Under the Business Corporations Act, the address of the attorney or his or her place of business is where service is effected.

The attorney who consents to act must sign the Notice of Attorney. This individual need not be a solicitor but must be an Alberta resident and can be a resident Albertan corporation as long as a particular individual is specified as the corporate representative. (See Sample #50.)

The foreign jurisdiction company must obtain certified copies of its incorporating documents and any subsequent amendments to them. The incorporating documents are the documents used to incorporate the company.

In Alberta, for example, the incorporating documents are simply the Articles of Incorporation plus the Certificate of Incorporation and any amendments to them that have been filed.

Those documents can be ordered from the Registrar of Companies in the originating province, who can provide what are called "certified copies" of those documents. In certain circumstances, if you have true copies of the documents in your possession, and you can obtain a notarial certificate from a notary public who can swear in writing that the attached copies are true copies of the originals, then those documents may be accepted. Sample #51 shows a notarial certificate for West Coast Publishing. However, to be on the safe side, you should order certified copies of the documents from the relevant provincial Registrar. They can usually be obtained within two weeks.

Finally, a Certificate of Status from the incorporating jurisdiction is required. A Certificate of Status is a certificate from the Registrar of Companies of the incorporating jurisdiction indicating that the company is in good standing in the province that it was originally incorporated in.

If a company is deficient in any of its filings, the Certificate of Status will not be granted and you will be delayed in registering extra-provincially. This is obviously another good reason to keep all corporate filings up to date. A Certificate of Status is shown in Sample #52.

The documents and the filing fee of $300 should be submitted to the Corporate Registry at the address listed on page 42.

(b) Attorney

The attorney for the company is, as stated above, the representative of the foreign jurisdiction company. The attorney need not necessarily be a lawyer or any other professional, but can be a representative of the company even if a salesperson or a rental agent.

The attorney really incurs no liability by acting in this capacity except to the extent that legal documents may be served on the attorney or the attorney's office. Therefore, once served with the legal documents, it is necessary for the attorney to tell the head office that a legal action has been started. If the attorney fails to do so, there may be some liability against the attorney on the basis of negligence.

If an attorney dies or resigns, the extra-provincial company must send to the Registrar, again on Form 27, a change of attorney notification, so that at all times the foreign jurisdiction company has an attorney in this province. Failure to have an attorney here invalidates the registration of the company. A Notice of Change of Address of Registered Attorney, Form 27.1, (see Sample #53) must be sent to the Registrar if the attorney's address changes.

(c) Name

Perhaps the most difficult problem involved in the registration of an extra-provincial company is the approval of the name in Alberta. The situation often arises where a name has been validly approved for the company in another jurisdiction and it has carried on business in that jurisdiction with that name. The company develops a certain amount of goodwill and it naturally wants to continue using its name when it does business in Alberta.

However, if another company has already used that name or a similar name in Alberta, it is unavailable. The Business Corporations Act allows a foreign jurisdiction company to use a pseudonym if the original name is not acceptable in Alberta. Acceptance of the name is based on the criteria discussed in chapter 2. (The assumed name cannot be a name of an existing Alberta corporation, or one that has been reserved for a future corporation.)

This practice allows the corporation to register in Alberta without having to change its name. It must, however, acquire all of its property and rights in Alberta under the assumed name. It is entitled to all property and rights acquired with that name and may be sued or sue in its name or the assumed name.

West Coast Publishing Ltd. ran into this problem because there was a company in Alberta registered with the name West Coast

SAMPLE #49
STATEMENT OF REGISTRATION
OF EXTRA-PROVINCIAL CORPORATION

BUSINESS CORPORATIONS ACT
EXTRA-PROVINCIAL CORPORATIONS
(SECTION 267)

FORM 24

Alberta
CONSUMER AND
CORPORATE AFFAIRS

STATEMENT OF REGISTRATION

1. NAME OF CORPORATION.	2. DATE OF INCORPORATION, AMALGAMATION OR CONTINUANCE.
B & K WEST COAST PUBLISHING LTD.	August 17, 1985

3. PLACE OF INCORPORATION, AMALGAMATION OR CONTINUANCE.

Vancouver, British Columbia

4. HEAD OFFICE ADDRESS INSIDE OR OUTSIDE ALBERTA.

#336, 15 Howe Street   Vancouver, British Columbia   Z1P 0G0

5. PRINCIPAL BUSINESS OF CORPORATION.

Publishing and sale of novels

6. DIRECTORS OF CORPORATION.

NAME	ADDRESS
Arthur Author	1724 West 15th Avenue, Vancouver, B.C. Z1P 0G0
Eddie Editor	1627 Granville Street, Vancouver, B.C. Z1P 0G0

7. WAS THIS CORPORATION EVER INCORPORATED OR PREVIOUSLY REGISTERED IN ALBERTA? ☐ YES ☒ NO

IF **YES**, UNDER WHAT NAME AND CORPORATE ACCESS NUMBER WAS IT INCORPORATED/REGISTERED.

CORPORATE NAME	ACCESS NUMBER

8. IS THIS CORPORATION VALID AND SUBSISTING IN ITS HOME JURISDICTION? ☒ YES ☐ NO

9. DATE	SIGNATURE	TITLE
May 10, 199-	*Arthur Author*	President

FOR DEPARTMENTAL USE ONLY

FILED

CORPORATE ACCESS NO.

CCA-06.124
(REV. 8/85)

W

SAMPLE #50
NOTICE OF ATTORNEY FOR SERVICE

IMPORTANT: PLEASE READ INSTRUCTIONS ON THE BACK OF THIS FORM.

BUSINESS CORPORATIONS ACT
(SECTIONS 267 AND 275)

FORM 27

Alberta
CONSUMER AND
CORPORATE AFFAIRS

NOTICE OF ATTORNEY FOR SERVICE OR CHANGE OF ATTORNEY OR ALTERNATIVE ATTORNEY

1. NAME OF CORPORATION:	2. ALBERTA CORPORATE ACCESS NUMBER:
B & K WEST COAST PUBLISHING LTD.	24682468

3.
- ☒ ATTORNEY
- ☐ CHANGE OF ATTORNEY
- ☐ ALTERNATIVE ATTORNEY
- ☐ CHANGE OF ALTERNATIVE ATTORNEY
- ☐ RESIGNATION/REVOCATION OF _____ AS ALTERNATIVE ATTORNEY
  (NAME)

4. THE ABOVE-MENTIONED CORPORATION HAS APPOINTED   STEW COOKE
(MUST BE AN INDIVIDUAL)

AS THE CORPORATION'S ATTORNEY FOR SERVICE.

5. FULL ADDRESS, INCLUDING POSTAL CODE, OF ATTORNEY. (POST OFFICE BOX **NOT** SUFFICIENT).

9735 Wealthy Drive S.W., Calgary, Alberta Z1P 0G0

6. I, STEW COOKE _____ HEREBY CONSENT TO ACT AS THE

ATTORNEY OF THE ABOVE-NAMED CORPORATION.

DATED THIS ___10th___ DAY OF ___May___ 19_9-_

SIGNATURE ___Stew Cooke___

WITNESS:
SIGNATURE ___Carmel Cooke___

NAME ___Carmel Cooke___

ADDRESS ___9735 Wealthy Drive S.W., Calgary, Alberta Z1P 0G0___

7. DATE	SIGNATURE	TITLE
May 10, 199-	B.B. Brooke B & K West Coast Publishing Ltd.	President TELEPHONE NUMBER 247-5689
FOR DEPARTMENTAL USE ONLY		FILED
THIS FORM WILL BE REJECTED IF NOT PROPERLY COMPLETED		

CC-06 127

132

Stationery & Printing Ltd. The company felt that the two names were so similar as to cause some public confusion. It was therefore necessary for West Coast Publishing Ltd. to carry on under an assumed name. The assumed name that was approved was B & K West Coast Publishing Ltd., which is the name that appears on the filing documents.

Although a federal corporation has a priority regarding names, it must also use a pseudonym if it wants to register extra-provincially in Alberta and its name is too similar or otherwise confusing with an existing Alberta corporation.

(d) Amendments

If a company amends its incorporating documents in its home jurisdiction, those amendments must also be filed in the province of Alberta. They must be sent within one month of the effective date of the change and be accompanied by either a notice on Form 28 if the change relates to a change of head office or a copy of the actual amendment to the charter document.

West Coast Publishing changed the address of its head office. Sample #54 shows Form 28 if filed in Alberta.

2. Certificate of Registration

Once all the necessary documents and fees are submitted, the Registrar of Companies will issue to the extra-provincial company a Certificate of Registration. The Certificate of Registration for B & K West Coast Publishing Ltd. is shown in Sample #55.

Like the Certificate of Incorporation, the Certificate of Registration of an extra-provincial corporation is conclusive proof that the company has validly registered in the province of Alberta as of the date shown in the certificate. The company is then entitled to all the rights and benefits of a company registered in the province of Alberta as far as an extra-provincial company is concerned. Please remember, however, that the basic rights of shareholders,

directors, etc., will be determined by the laws of the jurisdiction where the company was first incorporated, and not by Alberta law.

3. Annual Return

An extra-provincial company is required to file an Annual Return (Form 22). The information required is basically the same as the information that was originally required, such as the name and address of the attorney, name of the corporation, and place of incorporation. (See Sample #56.) There is a $20 filing fee.

Failure to file the Annual Return will result in some severe consequences. A company that does not file on time is subject to being dissolved by the Registrar. If that happens, the company will be forced to go through the revival procedure to again become properly registered in the province of Alberta.

The Business Corporations Act also requires that a corporation send to the Registrar any other information that the Registrar reasonably requires.

4. Validity of acts

The simple fact that a foreign jurisdiction company is not registered in Alberta will not, because of non-registration, invalidate transactions carried on by that company.

For example, if a foreign jurisdiction company from British Columbia purchases property in Alberta prior to being registered here, the simple fact that it is not registered will not negate the contract for purchase of the property. However, the Land Titles Act of Alberta (which is the statute that governs land registrations in Alberta) does not allow registration of land in the name of a company that is not registered under the Business Corporations Act.

To enforce its rights in court, a foreign jurisdiction company will have to become registered in Alberta. It is made quite clear in the Business Corporations Act that an extra-provincial company is not capable of beginning or maintaining a lawsuit in Alberta unless it is registered.

However, as long as the corporation registers prior to beginning the action or, in some cases, even subsequent to beginning the action, the lawsuit may be maintained without loss of rights.

5. Ceasing to carry on business in Alberta

When an extra-provincial company ceases to carry on business in Alberta, it must send a notice to the Registrar. The Registrar then can cancel the registration after 90 days' notice and after publishing notice in the Registrar's periodical.

As already indicated, the Registrar may cancel the registration of an extra-provincial corporation if it is in default for a period of one year in sending to the Registrar any fee, notice, or document required, or if that extra-provincial company contravenes any of the other relevant sections of the Business Corporations Act.

c. REGISTERING ALBERTA COMPANIES IN A FOREIGN JURISDICTION

If you have incorporated your company in Alberta and want to carry on your business in other provinces as well as Alberta, you are entitled to register your company in one or more of the other corporate jurisdictions in Canada.

The procedure for registering the company will be very similar to the procedure just discussed for registering foreign jurisdiction companies in Alberta. However, you should refer to the law of each particular jurisdiction in order to determine exactly what is required. In all cases, you will have to submit certified copies of the incorporating documents for the company. So you should order from the Registrar certified copies of your Articles of Incorporation and Certificate of Incorporation.

If your company was incorporated prior to February 1, 1982, the incorporating documents you need are the Articles of Association, the Memorandum of Association, and the Certificate of Incorporation.

You will also have to appoint an attorney or a representative in the foreign jurisdiction to act on your behalf in accepting service of legal documents. Many jurisdictions want complete details of the share structure and capital of the company, and some ask how much of the share capital will be used in the province. Finally, a filing fee in each jurisdiction will have to be paid.

For more detailed information about the filing requirements in other provinces, see the incorporation guides published by Self-Counsel Press for B.C., Saskatchewan, Manitoba, and Ontario.

d. CONTINUING A FOREIGN COMPANY AS AN ALBERTA COMPANY

Under certain circumstances, a company may not want to register a company extra-provincially in Alberta, but simply transfer the jurisdiction of the company from the foreign jurisdiction to Alberta. In effect, therefore, Alberta becomes the new incorporating jurisdiction, and subject to Alberta laws only.

To allow this type of jurisdictional transfer, the Registrar must be satisfied that the laws of the other jurisdiction authorize this procedure. Some provinces in Canada, such as Manitoba and Ontario, do not make provision for this type of transfer and some, such as Quebec, do not allow companies to be transferred into other jurisdictions.

You will have to examine the requirements in each particular jurisdiction in order to determine whether or not your company's base can be transferred.

SAMPLE #51
NOTARIAL CERTIFICATE

NOTARIAL CERTIFICATE

CANADA   )
PROVINCE OF ALBERTA   )
    TO WIT:)

    I, DAVID M. GOLDENBERG, of the City of Calgary, in the Province of Alberta, a Notary Public by royal authority duly appointed, DO CERTIFY that the paper writing hereto annexed are true copies of documents produced and shown to me from the custody of ARTHUR AUTHOR, President of B & K West Coast Publishing Ltd. and purporting to be true copies of the:

    (a) Certificate of Incorporation

    (b) Certificate of Change of Name

    (c) Memorandum

    (d) Articles

of B & K West Coast Publishing Ltd., the said copies having been compared by me with the original document an act whereof being requested, I have granted under my notarial form and seal of office to serve as occasion shall or may required.

                IN TESTIMONY WHEREOF I have hereunto subscribed my name and affixed myseal of office at the City of Calgary, in the Province of Alberta, this 5th day of May, 199- .

_____
A Notary Public in and for the Province of Alberta

135

13,579

Certificate
"COMPANY ACT"

Canada
Province of British Columbia

I Hereby Certify *that* according to the records of this office

"B & K WEST COAST PUBLISHING LTD. "

a Company duly incorporated under the laws of the Province of British

Columbia is an existing Corporation and is with respect to filing of

returns, in good standing.

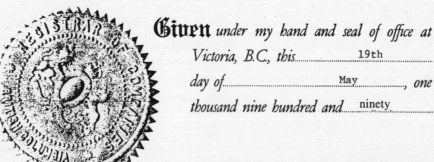

Given *under my hand and seal of office at*
Victoria, B.C., this................19th
day of..............May................, *one*
thousand nine hundred and ninety

....
Registrar of Companies.

Per: "I.M. Registrar"
Signing Officer

SAMPLE #53
NOTICE OF CHANGE OF ADDRESS
OF REGISTERED ATTORNEY

BUSINESS CORPORATIONS ACT
(SECTION 275 (5))

FORM 27.1

Alberta CONSUMER AND CORPORATE AFFAIRS

**NOTICE OF CHANGE OF
ADDRESS OF REGISTERED ATTORNEY**

1. NAME OF CORPORATION:	2. CORPORATE ACCESS NUMBER:
B & K WEST COAST PUBLISHING LTD.	24682468

3. NAME OF REGISTERED ATTORNEY:

STEW COOKE

4. NEW ADDRESS:

1015 Full Plate Lane, Calgary Alberta, Z1P CGO

5. EFFECTIVE DATE OF CHANGE:

September 15, 199-

6. DATE	SIGNATURE	TITLE
August 1, 199-	*B. B. Brooke*	President
FOR DEPARTMENTAL USE ONLY		FILED

CCA-06.127.1
(Rev 06/89)

If the other jurisdiction does provide for it, the Registrar of Companies, upon receiving all the information required, will issue a Certificate of Continuance which deems the company to be registered under the province of Alberta as if it has been incorporated under Alberta law.

You must file with the Registrar Articles of Continuance and a Notice of Directors and Notice of Address.

The date on the Certificate of Continuance which will be issued by the Registrar will be the date on which the corporation is deemed to become a corporation under the Business Corporations Act as if it had been incorporated at that date under the Business Corporations Act.

Any property held by the company prior to this continuation will continue to be the property of the company, and the company will continue to have all of the obligations and liabilities that it had prior to continuation. Therefore, a company cannot "lose" any of its debts or liabilities by moving from jurisdiction to jurisdiction.

Similarly, shares of the company issued prior to registration will maintain all rights after registration. This may be the only time when par value shares will be accepted in the province of Alberta.

e. CONTINUING AN ALBERTA COMPANY AS A FOREIGN COMPANY

For the same reasons as noted above, an Alberta company may wish to continue in business as a company incorporated in another jurisdiction, whether federal or provincial. This is also provided for under the Business Corporations Act.

The shareholders of the Alberta company will have to agree in special resolution to continue in the foreign jurisdiction. This type of resolution qualifies as a fundamental change, so the rights and remedies of the shareholders who dissent must be taken into consideration.

In addition, the Registrar of Companies must be satisfied that the continuance in another jurisdiction will not adversely affect creditors or shareholders of the corporation. In other words, the Registrar does have the authority to turn down the shareholders' request to continue elsewhere. In most cases, the Registrar will issue a letter saying that there is no objection to the transfer of jurisdiction for the company.

At the shareholders' meeting, all of the shareholders are entitled to vote on the continuation even if the shares are normally non-voting shares. Once all the requirements are provided for, the Registrar will issue a Certificate of Discontinuance and the corporation becomes an extra-provincial corporation as if it had been incorporated under the laws of the other jurisdiction.

As with the continuation of a foreign company in Alberta, the Registrar will not allow a continuation of an Alberta company in a foreign jurisdiction unless all of the property rights and share rights continue unchanged.

Check the jurisdiction where you want to be continued to find out if there are additional requirements. You certainly will have to obtain certified copies of your registration documents and probably a consent in writing from the Alberta Registrar.

SAMPLE #54
NOTICE OF CHANGE OF HEAD OFFICE (FORM 28)

BUSINESS CORPORATIONS ACT
EXTRA-PROVINCIAL CORPORATIONS
(SECTION 276)

FORM 28

Alberta

CONSUMER AND
CORPORATE AFFAIRS

NOTICE OF CHANGE OF HEAD OFFICE

1. NAME OF CORPORATION.	2. CORPORATE ACCESS NO.
B & K WEST COAST PUBLISHING LTD.	24682468

3. NEW ADDRESS OF THE HEAD OFFICE INSIDE OR OUTSIDE ALBERTA.

16716 - 3rd Avenue, Richmond, British Columbia   Z1P 0G0

4. EFFECTIVE DATE OF CHANGE.

January 14, 199-

5. DATE	SIGNATURE	TITLE
January 21, 199-	*Stew Cooke*	Attorney

FOR DEPARTMENTAL USE ONLY

w

CERTIFICATE OF REGISTRATION

BUSINESS CORPORATIONS ACT
FORM 25
CERTIFICATE OF REGISTRATION
EXTRA-PROVINCIAL CORPORATION

B & K WEST COAST PUBLISHING LTD.   24682468
Name of Corporation   Corporate Access No.

I hereby certify that the above-mentioned corporation, the Statement of Registration of which is attached, was registered as an Extra-Provincial Corporation under the Business Corporations Act of the Province of Alberta.

Registrar   Date of Registration

I. M. Registrar

AUDIT

SAMPLE #56
ANNUAL RETURN FOR EXTRA-PROVINCIAL CORPORATION

Alberta

Business Corporations Act

Form 22.1

ANNUAL RETURN

Consumer and Corporate Affairs Corporate Registry	8th Floor 10365 - 97 Street Edmonton, Alberta T5J 3W7 (403) 427-2311	902 J.J. Bowlen Bldg. 620 - 7 Avenue S.W. Calgary, Alberta T2P 0Y8 (403) 297-3442

① CORPORATE ACCESS NO. **01234567**   ② FOR THE YEAR ENDING 19 **9-**

③ DATE OF INCORPORATION, CONTINUANCE, AMALGAMATION

④ CORPORATION NAME   OR REGISTRATION: **9- 05 12**
                                              YY   MM   DD

B & K WEST COAST PUBLISHING LTD.

⑤ ADDRESS **#336, 15 Howe Street Vancouver, B.C.   Z1P 0G0**

⑥ HAS THERE BEEN A CHANGE OF DIRECTORS?   YES ☐ NO ☒
⑦ IF YES, HAS FORM 6 BEEN PREVIOUSLY   FILED ☐ or ATTACHED ☐
⑧ DOES THIS CORPORATION OWN CONTROLLED LAND   YES ☐ NO ☒
⑨ IS THE CORPORATION CURRENTLY ENGAGED IN ANY ACTIVITIES WHICH MAY RESULT IN RECEIPT OF REVENUE OF ANY KIND?   YES ☒ NO ☐

⑩ SHAREHOLDERS   % OF VOTING SHARES ISSUED

NAME **Arthur Author**
ADDRESS **1724 West 15th Avenue**
        Vancouver, B.C. Z1P 0G0

CORPORATE ACCESS NUMBER **01234567**   **51** %

NAME **Eddie Editor**
ADDRESS **1627 Granville Street**
        Vancouver, B.C. Z1P 0G0

CORPORATE ACCESS NUMBER **01234568**   **49** %

NAME
ADDRESS

CORPORATE ACCESS NUMBER _____   ___ %

NAME
ADDRESS

CORPORATE ACCESS NUMBER _____   ___ %

NAME
ADDRESS

CORPORATE ACCESS NUMBER _____   ___ %

INSTRUCTIONS FOR COMPLETION OF THIS FORM ON REVERSE SIDE

⑪ DATE **May 15, 199-**	⑫ SIGNATURE *Arthur Author*	⑬ TELEPHONE NO. **987-6543**	⑭ FILED

CCA-06 122.1
(REV. 1/87)

8
ACCOUNTING AND TAX CONSIDERATIONS

a. INTRODUCTION

Once a company is properly off and running, the legal considerations, except in extraordinary situations, become secondary to the actual operation of the business. The operation of the business consists of generating income, keeping proper and accurate records, and, ultimately, planning for your taxes.

This chapter discusses briefly how your financial records should be set up initially, the types of statements that your creditors and lenders will be looking at when it comes time for you to borrow money or obtain credit, and some tips on where and what to look for in an accountant. It also examines some of the tax considerations involved in operating your company.

b. KEEPING YOUR FINANCIAL RECORDS

1. Day-to-day record keeping

From the time that you make the decision to carry on business, whether as an incorporated company or otherwise, it is essential that you keep proper records of all expenditures and income. These records are necessary not only for filing tax returns and ensuring that you are paying the least amount of tax possible, but also to allow you to assess how the company is doing in terms of expenses, revenue, and net profit.

There are many systems available that allow you to keep these records. They range from very simple methods of keeping a journal and entering all transactions in that journal, to more sophisticated systems known as fail safe or one-write accounting systems that provide you with checks and balances on all the expenses incurred by the business.

At the most basic level, I suggest that you first do the following things:

(a) Set up a separate bank account to be used by your business only; if it is a corporation, you will have to obtain the necessary corporate banking forms and fill them out. See chapter 4 for a discussion of how that is done. Obtain separate cheques for use exclusively in the business.

(b) Obtain and prepare a daily journal where you can enter all expenditures and income as well as keep a current balance of the account at all times.

(c) Ensure that all monies you are using in the business flow through the bank account so that an appropriate record is maintained in the bank statement. For example, if you are personally going to lend $1 000 to the company, do not simply take $1 000 out of your account and use it to purchase something for the business; put the $1 000 from your personal account into your corporate account and write a corporate cheque for the item you are acquiring. Ensure that the appropriate documents are prepared as evidence of your loan of $1 000 to the company.

(d) Learn how to reconcile your bank statement with your daily journal in order to ensure that all of the entries that the bank makes are accurate.

(e) Set up a preliminary filing system that allows you to file all documents related to the business in such a manner that they are readily available to you.

(f) Obtain the services of a good bookkeeper or accountant. (See section c. below.)

2. Annual statements

At least once a year, it is customary to prepare two forms of financial statements to provide you with current financial information about your business. These are known as the balance sheet and the profit and loss statement. These two statements can provide both you and your creditors and lenders with valuable and current information about the company. These statements will also be required from time to time by lenders when you wish to borrow monies or obtain credit on behalf of the company.

The balance sheet is a statement of the company's asset and liability position as of a particular time. Sample #57 shows a balance sheet for Highrise Restaurants Ltd. as at August 31, 199-, which is the fiscal (financial) year end of the company.

The balance sheet shows what is owned and owed by the company at a particular time. There are three sections to the balance sheet: assets, liabilities, and retained earnings.

The assets are normally listed in the left-hand column of the statement and are broken down into various classifications ranging from those assets which are most liquid (i.e., cash on hand) to those assets which are least liquid (i.e., kitchen equipment).

Current assets are those assets which will normally be used up within one year of the current balance sheet date. All fixed assets are those assets which will provide longer-term benefits to the company.

The assets are valued normally to the lower of their original cost or market cost. Therefore, the land owned by the company is valued on the balance sheet at $50 000 even though it may, in fact, be worth considerably more on the open market.

The balance sheet also shows that some of the assets, notably the kitchen equipment, have a depreciated value. The income tax department allows you to depreciate certain assets at a particular rate in order to reflect in some way the fact that these assets do not last forever and over a period of time will wear out and require replacement.

The amount of the depreciable value is an expense against the income of the company and, therefore, only the depreciated value of the asset is listed on the balance sheet. Because the asset may eventually be sold for more than the original cost, the difference between the book value of that asset (the value shown on the balance sheet) and the sale price will be known as recapture and will have to be included in the income of the company.

The liability side of the balance sheet basically follows a similar pattern to the asset side of the balance sheet. It lists those liabilities which are short-term down to liabilities which include long-term debt and are payable over a longer period of time.

The difference between the assets and liabilities is known as the retained earnings of the company. The retained earnings include the initial share investment of the company and the net profit. Accordingly, if the retained earnings show a deficit, it is clear that at that time, the company is losing money.

In the case of Highrise Restaurants Ltd., the initial share contribution was $2 700. Because the retained earnings figure is now $15 700, the balance sheet shows that the company has earned a profit as at August 31, 199-, in the amount of $13 000.

The balance sheet should itemize each particular class of share because the Business Corporations Act requires that each class of share have its own account.

The second statement prepared for the company is known as the profit and loss statement. (See Sample #58.) This statement indicates the profit or loss of the company over a period of time. Unlike the balance sheet, the profit and loss statement is a statement over a period of time and not as at a particular point in time.

It does, however, tell us the profit or loss of the company by subtracting the total expenses incurred in a period from the total revenue earned in that period. The profit should equal the profit portion of the retained earnings section on the balance sheet.

In the profit and loss statement, the various expenses of the company are itemized, such as food costs, interest costs, rental costs, etc., and the revenue is also broken down into the revenue generated from the sale of food, from the sale of beverages, and from miscellaneous revenue which include sales from cigarette machines, etc.

The preparation and interpretation of both of these statements is an art that accountants spend many, many years perfecting. It is not unlikely that, faced with these statements for the first time in your life, you will have some difficulty not only in preparing them but in understanding what they say. In fact, these statements can be written up in so many ways that they can say a number of different things to a number of different people and are really only an imperfect tool. However, they are accepted in the business world and, in fact, an audited financial statement is basically a statement that a chartered accountant is prepared to stake his or her professional reputation on.

My advice is that unless you have had some previous experience, you do not prepare your own financial statements at first. There are a number of software programs that are currently available to assist you in setting up financial records, and even in preparing basic financial statements. Normally, when your business is just getting off the ground, the preparation of the statements will not be expensive as long as you have kept proper and accurate books on a regular basis. The question then becomes who to choose to prepare these statements.

c. WHO TO CHOOSE FOR AN ACCOUNTANT

It is extremely difficult to recommend any particular class of accountant because their expertise may vary from business to business. Just as in other professions, some accountants are more expert in working with one type of business or another.

You should make inquiries to find out the names of some accountants who are familiar with the type of business that you are carrying on. I recommend that you consult with others in similar businesses, with your lawyer, or with the association or group involved in your business.

There are different categories of accountants. The most commonly known category is the chartered accountant. Chartered accountants normally have a university degree in business or commerce and have also taken extensive courses offered by the Institute of Chartered Accountants and passed some very gruelling exams. There are national firms of chartered accountants carrying on business in Alberta as well as many smaller firms consisting of one, two, or three people.

Chartered accountants have considerable academic knowledge and a good understanding of the complicated tax laws that affect your business. However, chartered accountants normally charge a higher hourly fee than other accountants and, especially in the larger firms, you may find that they are not prepared to take on a small operation.

144

SAMPLE #57
BALANCE SHEET

BALANCE SHEET HIGHRISE RESTAURANTS LTD.
as at August 31st, 199-

ASSETS			LIABILITIES		
Current:			Current:		
Cash on hand in Bank		$ 5 000.00	Trade Accounts Payable		$ 5 000.00
Account Receivable (less allowance for doubtful debt)		1 600.00	Accrued Wages		1 000.00
Merchandise Inventory (Food and Beverages)		2 500.00	Employees Tax Payable		500.00
Prepaid Expenses		2 000.00			
TOTAL CURRENT ASSETS:		$ 11 100.00	TOTAL CURRENT LIABILITIES		$ 6 500.00
Fixed (at cost):			Fixed (long term):		
Land		$ 50 000.00	Bank loan (operating)		$ 40 000.00
Building	$ 20 000.00		Land Mortgage		19 100.00
less deprec.	1 000.00		Taxes Payable		3 000.00
		19 000.00	Due to Shareholder		20 000.00
Vehicles	6 000.00		TOTAL FIXED:		$ 82 100.00
less deprec.	1 800.00				
		4 200.00			
Store fixtures & kitchen equipment	25 000.00		RETAINED EARNINGS		
less deprec.	5 000.00		Capital Stock outstanding		
		20 000.00	100 Class "A"		100.00
TOTAL FIXED		$ 93 200.00	100 Class "B"		100.00
			50 Class "E"		2 500.00
TOTAL ASSETS		$104 300.00	Earned Surplus		13 000.00
			TOTAL RETAINED EARNINGS		$ 15 700.00
			TOTAL LIABILITIES & RETAINED EARNINGS		$104 300.00

SAMPLE #58
PROFIT AND LOSS STATEMENT

PROFIT AND LOSS STATEMENT
HIGHRISE RESTAURANTS LTD.
(April 1, 199- to August 31, 199-)

REVENUE		EXPENSES	
Food Sales	$ 36 000.00	Cost of Food	$ 20 600.00
Liquor Sales	10 000.00	Cost of Beverages	5 000.00
Miscellaneous sales	28 000.00	Salaries/Wages	12 500.00
(cigarette & takeout food)		Bank interest and	
Interest	750.00	principal paid	15 000.00
		Accounting	1 000.00
		Legal	150.00
		Maintenance of equipment	
		& vehicles	2 500.00
		Advertising	3 000.00
		Replacement of	
		inventory	2 000.00
		TOTAL EXPENSES	$ 61,750.00
TOTAL REVENUE	$ 74 750.00		

Total Revenue	$ 74 750.00	
Less total expense	61 750.00	
	$ 13 000.00	

Other types of accountants are known as certified general accountants (CGAs) and certified management accountants (CMAs). Both groups have obtained a form of recognized certification after having taken courses either through a technical institute or private correspondence. Depending on the nature of your business, they may be more suitable for your needs.

Each group of accountants has its own governing body which maintains offices in Alberta. Information about the various fields each particular accounting group has expertise in can be obtained from the governing body for that group.

Bookkeeping services are an inexpensive source of accounting assistance. These services provide companies with assistance in their day-to-day record keeping and also in the preparation and filing of corporate tax returns. Programs for personal computers are widely available, and can assist you in keeping track of your financial transactions.

Lending institutions, investors, or creditors may require audited financial statements from your company from time to time. These should only be prepared by professional accountants who act as independent examiners of the records of the company. They then prepare financial statements certified as correct. These audited statements serve to provide comfort to lenders and investors who are entitled to rely on the statements as true and accurate.

In the early stages of your company it is probably unlikely that you are going to need the services of a chartered or other professional accountant. The money is probably better spent taking a few basic accounting courses or acquiring some books and software on how to keep records for your company. In the long run, this will not only assist you in keeping your expenses down when it comes time to file your tax returns, but it also will give you the knowledge necessary to communicate with accountants on their level so you will understand what they are doing and how they are doing it. See *Basic Accounting for the Small Business* and *Understanding and Managing Financial Information,* two other titles in the Self-Counsel Series.

As your company grows and you start becoming more and more involved with lenders and creditors, you will probably have to opt for a higher level of accounting service, which may or may not include a chartered accountant.

Like every other service industry, accountants must produce in order to maintain your confidence and your business.

Once you have retained the services of an accounting firm that has the expertise you require and also has your confidence, you will find that the accountant can be a very valuable asset in the operation of your business.

d. TAX ADVANTAGES TO INCORPORATING

There can be substantial tax advantages to incorporating your business. This section outlines the major ones.

1. Basic corporate rate

The basic combined federal and provincial corporate income tax rate before the small business deduction and manufacturing and processing credit is currently approximately 44%. The rate on income from manufacturing operations is about 40%. The rate on manufacturing income is now about 39%.

2. Qualifying for the small business tax rate

First, provided your business can qualify for the small business rate, there is a substantial reduction in taxes payable on business earnings. Currently the rate in Alberta is about 22% on the first $200 000 of net income from active business.

To qualify for the small business rate on the first $200 000 of net income from an *active* business, there are two basic tests to meet:

(a) Your corporation must be a Canadian-controlled private corporation; that is, a private Canadian corporation other than a corporation controlled directly or indirectly by one or more non-residents or by one or more public corporations or by any such combination.

(b) Your company must generate income from an active business in Canada.

If the corporation fails both tests, then the tax rate will be between approximately 40% and 49% depending on whether the income is from manufacturing. Any business carried on by your company will be considered active with two exceptions: personal services businesses (which refers to personal services that would ordinarily be provided by an individual employee rather than by a company) and investment businesses. Companies that carry on these two kinds of business will be taxed at the top corporate rate. Furthermore, a company carrying on a personal services business (sometimes referred to as an "incorporated employee") will not be allowed all the deductions available to other companies.

These two exceptions to the active business rules will not, however, apply if the company has six or more full-time employees throughout the year, or, in the case of a management service company, it receives its income from a corporation associated with it. In such cases, investment companies and "incorporated employees" will both be eligible for the low tax rate.

Assuming you qualify for the small business rate, the tax advantages to incorporation are outlined below.

3. Minimize non-deductible or depreciable expenses

Second, you realize an immediate tax savings by doing it yourself, and this is over and above the straight cost savings. This is because lawyer's and Registrar's fees for incorporation are not wholly tax deductible as an expense. (They are tax deductible only to the extent of 70% of the expenditure on a 10% declining balance basis.)

Further, they are not even depreciable as most assets are. The money you spend on incorporating remains on the balance sheet forever as an undepreciated asset.

4. Split your income

Third, with a company you can effectively "split" your income. For example, say your business made $50 000 last year as a proprietorship. This entire amount would be considered your personal income and be taxed at a rate of approximately 50%.

On the other hand, if you have incorporated, $25 000 could be paid to you personally as salary on bonus and $25 000 could be left in the company to use as you please. The $25 000 left in the company treasury would be taxed at the rate of 22% if your company qualifies for the small business tax rate.

On the $25 000 paid out to you personally you would pay tax in the 24% to 31% range depending on the number of personal deductions, etc.

This is just one example. In fact, you are allowed to work out any combination which keeps your total tax bill to a minimum, including employing members of your family, provided they are employed in a bona fide capacity and the payment is reasonable.

Currently, a qualifying company's tax rate is only 22% on all earnings below $200 000 in each year. Therefore, if your company's earnings are $50 000 a year, a further split is also possible after paying the 22% tax rate. After paying this initial corporate tax, you can then choose to either leave the funds in the company or pay out

dividends to the shareholders (you, your spouse, and children).

Depending upon other sources of income and your income tax bracket, it may be more advantageous for one or more of your family members to take payments from the company in the form of dividends alone or in a mixture of dividends and salary.

An individual (other than a resident of Quebec), with no other sources of income will be able to receive approximately $22 000 of Canadian dividends without being subject to tax. This is because of the dividend tax credit. However, the company must be properly structured in order for this technique to work properly.

However, since dividends are not deductible and it is important to limit, if at all possible, net corporate business income to $200 000 in order to pay the lowest corporate income tax rate, payments of bonuses and salary may be preferable to dividends.

One critical point to keep in mind is that dividend income does *not* qualify as "earned income" for purposes of making a deductible contribution to an RRSP. Thus, if your entire income consisted of dividends, you could not get a deduction for any contribution to your RRSP. Furthermore, your income might also be subject to the new minimum tax.

5. Estate planning benefits

With a company, you can effect substantial estate planning advantages. As this is a technical area and beyond the scope of this book, it will not be discussed at any length. Suffice it to say that the existence of a company enables you to own a widely diversified portfolio of assets (including all kinds of property) under the ownership of a single entity.

This can be a great advantage both from a tax and administrative point of view, especially if the company is located in a non-taxing jurisdiction like Alberta and the assets are located in a taxing jurisdiction.

6. Use salary and bonus accruals

Through a company, you can declare yourself a bonus that is deductible from the company's income but need not be declared by you as income until it is actually paid. However, the Income Tax Act has rules about how long you can delay declaring the payment as income to you. The rules say that the bonus has within 180 days from the end of your corporation's tax year in which the bonus was declared. For example, if your company's year end was January and you declared yourself a bonus of $10 000 on January 30, 1997, the company would deduct it as a salary expense for the 1996-97 year only if the bonus was actually paid by July 31, 1997. The result is that you would pay personal tax on the bonus in April, 1998 (less, of course, the tax the company would have to withhold when it paid you the bonus).

You can see that this gives you a fair amount of flexibility. To be deductible these bonuses must be reasonable (in relation to services rendered to the company) and represent a legal liability of the company. (Passing a directors' resolution is advisable.)

In addition, there are a number of other tax wrinkles and elections relating to the salary/dividend/bonus route which any competent tax advisor can tell you about.

The important thing to remember is that when planning bonuses, you must be careful to look at the overall tax liability of your company *and* you. If your company is already able to take advantage of the small business tax rate, there is little sense in declaring a bonus that will be taxed in your hands as income at a slightly higher rate.

If you want to reduce your company's earnings so that it can take advantage of the small business rate, you might want to declare a bonus payable to yourself, and wait before paying it to yourself. In this way you can "even out" the earnings and so pay less total tax over a period of years. For example, if you can foresee that your company's earnings for the fiscal year will exceed the amount eligible for the small business tax rate, declare a bonus for yourself as it may reduce the earnings sufficiently to enable the company to be taxed at the lower small business rate, or mean less money is taxable at a higher rate.

Furthermore, by reducing your corporate profits you reduce the size of the tax installment payments payable by the corporation and, therefore, improve your cash flow position.

If you declare dividends payable to yourself, there is no time limit on when they can be paid to you. Once the corporation has paid tax on its profits, dividends can be distributed at any time. This might be beneficial from the point of view of liability for personal income tax.

Remember, whichever method you choose to distribute your corporate earnings, it must be designed to meet the monetary needs and tax liability of both the company and yourself.

7. Expense deductions

Aside from the fact that operating through a limited company *may* allow you to claim more liberal entertainment and travel expenses, there are perfectly legal and sanctioned ways of using a company to increase expense allowances.

For example, country club and similar dues paid by your company on your behalf, while not tax deductible by the company, do not have to be included in your personal income. Therefore, because the company is taxed at a lower rate than you are personally, it can earn less than you personally to net the same amount.

However, business meals and entertainment are only deductible to the extent of 80% of their cost. The cost of business meals and entertainment subject to the 80% limitation includes gratuities, overcharges, room rentals at a hotel to provide entertainment, and tickets for various entertainment events.

Similarly, if you are arranging life insurance policies, the company can pay the premiums, (non-deductible — but the money earned to pay the premium is taxed at a lower rate) and any proceeds collected by you are non-taxable.

8. Planning for your retirement

In the past, the opportunity for small business owners to provide for their own retirement was exceptional. Unfortunately, that is no longer the case.

If you are an owner/employee of a corporation, you may not be a beneficiary of your corporation's deferred profit-sharing plan (DPSP). If the company does not have a DPSP or a registered pension plan (RPP), or you are not a beneficiary, your maximum contribution to a registered retirement savings plan (RRSP) can be $7 500 or 18% of your earned income, whichever is less.

Currently, your RRSP limit is $13 500 if you are not a member of a DPSP or an RPP.

9. Interest-free and low-interest loans to employees and shareholders

Loans made to employees are considered a taxable benefit and attract "imputed" interest income to the employee if made interest-free or below the "prescribed" loan rate set by the government. This rate is adjusted quarterly based on the interest paid on 91-day treasury bills for the previous quarter.

However, on loans to purchase shares in their employer company, employees may deduct the interest expense against all other employment income or income from property and dividends provided the shares bought are either preferred shares that yield taxable dividends higher than the prescribed interest rate paid or common shares. Thus, no benefit is included in the employee's income. Note, however, that to the extent that an employee's interest exceeds expense income from property

(e.g., interest and dividends, etc.) any immediate access to the capital gains exemption is effectively reduced by the amount of such excess until it is completely absorbed by income from the property.

If the loan is made to allow the employee to buy a car to be used on the job, the maximum deduction for interest costs is $250 per month. However, in order to deduct this maximum interest amount, you must drive your car not less than 24 000 kilometres per year. The rules pertaining to the deduction of automobile expenses are very complex, and your professional advisors should be consulted.

To summarize, low-interest or no-interest bearing loans to employees are not very beneficial unless they are made to allow the employee to buy shares of the employer's company. Loans to allow an employee to buy a car can be beneficial, but not to the same extent as share purchase loans.

10. Manufacturing and processing credit (M & P)

All active small business income is taxed at the same rate, and the rate on such income is about 22% for income earned in Alberta. The M & P credit reduces the income tax rate on manufacturing income not eligible for the small business rate to about 40%.

The M & P credit was introduced to reward labor intensive businesses, supposedly as a stimulus to employment. The Income Tax Act specifically excludes certain activities from qualifying. They are farming, fishing, logging, on-site job construction, most natural resource activities, and any manufacturing endeavor where manufacturing revenues are less than 10% of the gross sales.

A lot of businesses qualify that you wouldn't normally think would. For example, newspapers or any type of printing business would qualify. In fact, any business that changes, converts, adds to, or re-assembles the raw material may qualify.

11. Anti-avoidance

The federal government's general anti-avoidance rule means that any transaction that results in a significant reduction or even deferral of the tax that might have been payable had the transaction not occurred can be completely ignored unless it can be shown to have a bona fide non-tax purpose.

12. Conclusion

The realization that profits mean taxes tends to cause business people to overreact and become more and more committed to minimizing their tax load. This is totally understandable and perfectly acceptable, as long as the methods used are legal.

The best way of achieving the lowest possible taxes is to maintain proper and accurate records yourself and ensure that you have at your disposal the accounting expertise you require to assist you in taking advantage of all of the opportunities available under the current tax laws.

9
OTHER THINGS YOU SHOULD KNOW ABOUT RUNNING A SUCCESSFUL BUSINESS

a. GOVERNMENT REQUIREMENTS

For better or for worse, the three levels of government that control our destinies and deflate our pocketbooks are to a very large extent involved with your corporation. Business people often feel that they have taken on, involuntarily in most cases, a not-so-silent partner. However, the realities of the situation must be faced, and if you are to carry on a successful and prosperous business, the best approach is to be aware of the many and varied agencies that you may have to grapple with so that you can best minimize your cost and time involvement with them.

This chapter discusses briefly a number of the government agencies that may affect your business. In most cases, each of those agencies have their own public relations or public information departments, which can provide you with specific details on particular questions.

1. Federal requirements and regulations

The following are some federal agencies or programs that may affect your business.

(a) Goods and services tax

This goods and services tax (GST) is a form of value-added tax which is a concept common in Europe but new to North America. Under the GST, a business collects tax from all its customers. The tax is calculated as 7% of the sale price of the goods and services.

Each business is entitled to claim a credit for any tax paid on the purchase of goods or services used in its own business. This credit (an "input tax credit") is available to each business in the production and distribution chain except the final non-business consumer of the good or service. The final consumer, therefore, bears the full burden of the tax.

The total amount of the GST collected in a given period, typically quarterly, less the input tax credits for that period, must be remitted to Revenue Canada. If, in any given period, the input tax credit exceeds the tax collected on sales, a business will be entitled to a refund equal to the difference.

All businesses whose gross sales in the preceding year exceeded $30 000, are required to register with Revenue Canada — Customs and Excise for purposes of collecting and remitting GST on their sales. If a business' gross sales falls below the $30 000 threshold, registration is optional.

Unregistered businesses fall outside the GST net. They are not required to charge GST on their sales, but they are also unable to recover GST paid on their purchases. Therefore, even if sales are under $30 000 you should consider registering your corporation.

In order to claim the input tax credit, your corporation must keep detailed records of all GST charges made to it. It is very important to understand how to "track" all of your expenses and what adjustments to your accounting systems may be required. There are also a number of exceptions to the general rules that may affect your business.

(b) Federal excise tax

An excise tax, in addition to the goods and services tax, is imposed on certain specific goods, whether manufactured and produced in Canada or imported into Canada. The list of excisable items includes, among other things, jewellery, matches, cigarettes, and tobacco.

Complete details can be found in the Excise Tax Act, a copy of which may be ordered from the Canadian Government Publications Centre, Supply and Services Canada, Hull, Quebec, K1A 0S9. Some bookstores also carry copies of the act.

Revenue Canada — Customs and Excise requires that all persons or firms manufacturing or producing goods subject to an excise tax must operate under a manufacturer's excise tax licence, which can be obtained from the regional or district Excise Tax Office, Revenue Canada, in the area in which you or your company proposes to operate.

Manufacturers licensed for excise tax purposes may purchase or import, free from excise tax, goods that are to be incorporated into and form a constituent component part of an article that or product that is subject to an excise tax, provided they quote their excise tax licence number and relevant certificate.

(c) Customs duties

Any business that imports products from abroad must be aware of customs duties which are levied against goods upon entry into Canada.

There are regulations concerning invoicing, classification of goods, rates of duty, and reductions and exemptions for special classes of articles. It is advisable for you to obtain a ruling on the classification, rate of duty, and valuation prior to commencing shipments.

Foreign exporters and Canadian importers are advised to approach the regional collector of customs, Revenue Canada, having jurisdiction over the port of entry for the majority of their goods.

(d) Federal income tax

The federal government levies both personal and corporate income tax on monies earned in Canada. Income taxes are applied on income received or receivable during the taxation year from all sources, inside and outside Canada, less certain deductions.

Individuals and branches of foreign companies carrying on business in Canada are also liable for income taxes on profits derived from these business operations. Small businesses qualify for special tax rates (see chapter 8 on tax advantages for further information).

If you are an employer, you are required to deduct personal income tax from the pay cheques of all employees on a regular basis. You must remit these funds monthly through any branch of a chartered bank or to the Taxation Data Centre, Ottawa, Ontario.

Deduction of employee benefits must be made from the date of commencement of work. The federal income tax regulations outline the rules for allocating income to the provinces when individuals earn business income in more than one province.

For specific information about federal income tax, contact the nearest office of Revenue Canada — Taxation.

(e) Canada Pension Plan

If your company is an employer, it is necessary to make contributions to the Canada Pension Plan (CPP). The deductions must be made from the employees' salaries and matched with contributions from the employer. The funds must be remitted to Revenue Canada. Details can be obtained from your local taxation office.

As previously mentioned, directors may be personally liable for these remittances if the corporation does not pay them.

Note: If you are incorporated and pay yourself a wage, as far as the Canada Pension Plan is concerned you are not self-employed. You should deduct the normal amount from your wage and the company will also contribute as the employer.

(f) Employment insurance

Employers are also required to contribute to an employment insurance plan set up by the federal government. The plan is designed to provide benefits to individuals who find themselves in between jobs.

The employer is required to collect a contribution from each employee in accordance with certain rates and schedules provided by the tax department. Failure to make those payments will render the employer (and perhaps even the directors of the company) personally liable to contribute those monies out of corporate funds. Again, details should be obtained from your local taxation office.

Note: You may have heard of the concept of a "consulting company" as a vehicle to avoid payment of CPP and employment insurance benefits. A consulting company, if properly set up and validly used, can provide you with these types of tax planning benefits. However, it is necessary for you to prepare a written consulting agreement, and more important, meet the tests established by Revenue Canada.

(g) Investment Canada

This agency is designed to review transactions involving foreign parties. However, it deals with very large transactions and should not affect any matters your company will be involved with.

(h) Immigration laws

The federal government controls the area of law governing immigration. If you want to hire employees from abroad, you will have to deal with the immigration department. A point system has been developed to determine which foreigners may be allowed into Canada. One of the requirements of the system is that there be a job available that has been offered without success to Canadians.

You should also be aware that there are several programs in effect that may assist you in your business by providing for immigration investment and expertise. Full information can be obtained from the immigration officials in your area.

(i) Patents, copyrights, trade marks, and industrial designs

The items listed above are topics in an area of law known as intellectual property, not because it deals with things designed by people with extraordinarily brilliant minds, but because it represents types of property that, unlike chattels or land, have no real physical presence.

Therefore, the laws required to protect those types of assets have evolved differently from the laws created to protect other types of real and personal property.

These are all federally controlled and if your business involves any of these items, a registered patent or trade mark attorney may be consulted for assistance.

A patent is a right granted by the federal government to an inventor to exclude others from using that invention in Canada. The term of the patent is for 17 years and is granted for inventions that make some technological development or improvement not previously considered.

A copyright is the exclusive right of an author to reproduce every original literary, musical, dramatic, or artistic work he or she creates, provided the author is a Canadian citizen or a British subject or a citizen of a country that adheres to the Universal Copyright Convention. This right lasts for the life of the author plus 50 years after the author's death.

A trade mark is a symbol or design that may be registered to represent a particular service or good that the manufacturer is involved in. The trade mark lasts for 15 years and is renewable. It can also include trade names used by businesses.

An industrial design may be registered also. The registration provides the exclusive right to that design for a period of five years with an extension of one additional five-year period. A design protects a person who has conceived and expressed in a physical form an idea for something that is new or original in design.

The procedures involved in registering any of the above can be quite complicated because extensive searches have to be carried out in Ottawa. As well, the costs of registering any or all of these can be quite high. Before embarking on the registration procedure, you should check with a patent attorney and get an idea of the cost and time involved.

Remember that for an ordinary corporate name, these registrations are not required. If you are having difficulty determining if your business may be involved with one of the items above, a short call to your lawyer or to the relevant registration office should provide an answer.

* * *

The foregoing represents only a small number of federal government agencies and departments that may affect your business. Actually, you will probably be aware of those agencies that you deal with on a day-to-day basis. However, if you want to know about other federal government agencies that may be relevant to your business, see your accountant, lawyer, or banker, who may have that information.

2. Provincial requirements and regulations

There are a number of provincial government agencies that your business could come in contact with.

(a) Provincial income tax department

Under recent changes to the law, the province of Alberta now has jurisdiction for the administration and collection of corporate income tax. Accordingly, companies are required to file provincial income tax forms at the same time they file federal income tax forms. Sample #59 is a copy of an information sheet sent out by the provincial corporate tax department. This form will undoubtedly be sent to you shortly after incorporation; it should be properly filled in and submitted to the appropriate office as soon as possible.

(b) Workers' compensation

The Workers' Compensation Board has been set up to protect employees when accidents occur in the course of their employment.

The Workers' Compensation Board covers many varied types of employment. Most manual, labor, and industrial jobs are covered as well as provincial government jobs and retail jobs. The Board also has the power to bring an industry within the scope of its act, or exclude a particular trade or operation, such as farm or ranch workers.

Your company must register with the Workers' Compensation Board and make regular assessed payments to the Board. Those payments will be based on the number of employees and income of the company. Failure to pay those claims gives the Board a priority over many other creditors and may also give them the right to go after the corporate officers and directors for payment if the company does not pay the necessary assessments.

In return for the above, an employer will not have to pay employees for injuries they suffer while at work. The employer, however, must apply for this coverage and have the application approved by the Board. Employers are only bound to cover their employees, not independent contractors. In the construction industry, for example, contractors hire sub-trades as independent contractors, and so are not responsible for any Workers' Compensation Board assessments for those sub-trades. They would be responsible if, instead of subcontracting the jobs out, they had their own employees do the work.

Information regarding the application and the extent of coverage may be obtained from Workers' Compensation Offices throughout Alberta. Offices are located in Edmonton, Calgary, Red Deer, Lethbridge, and other centres throughout the province.

(c) Provincial licensing requirements

There are a number of Alberta laws and regulations that impose licensing requirements on individuals involved in certain businesses. Below is a list of those businesses, but you should check with your accountant, banker, or lawyer to determine if a licence is required in your particular business.

(a) Real estate sales (both of property inside and outside the province of Alberta)

(b) Sale of securities, stocks, bonds, etc.

(c) Door-to-door sales and direct sales; franchises

(d) Consumer financing companies

(e) Food processing

(f) Anyone involved in transportation including taxi drivers, chauffeurs, and transporters of goods, fish processing, and natural resources

(g) Hotel/restaurant facilities with or without licensed premises

The standards vary in each particular industry. In some cases, qualifying examinations are required while in others it is simply a matter of obtaining a licence after paying a registration fee. Further details can be obtained by contacting the appropriate provincial government office.

(d) Foreign land regulation controls

You should also be aware that there are some disclosure requirements regarding the acquisition of certain lands in the province of Alberta by individuals other than Alberta residents or Canadian citizens.

The lands in question are basically non-urban lands; refer to the exact regulations published by the provincial government in order to determine what those rights and prohibitions are.

* * *

There are a number of other provincial boards and tribunals that may in one way or another affect the type of business that you are carrying on. With the growth of government, business people may not be able to keep up with the vast proliferation of agencies, departments, and boards that almost seem to spring up overnight.

In order to stay current, try to find a group or organization formed by those who carry on a business similar to yours. These types of organizations can provide information that may not otherwise be available to you and can also provide other services that may be of immeasurable value to your business.

SAMPLE #59
TAX INFORMATION RETURN

Alberta Corporate Income Tax
Information Return: Corporate Identification

1 Alberta Corporate Tax Account Number: **15-FEB-**

Instructions: 21-222222-9

To receive the necessary forms, information and services to file your returns under THE ALBERTA CORPORATE INCOME TAX ACT, please ensure that the information requested below is:

1. complete and accurate;
2. consistent with information provided to Revenue Canada;
3. certified correct by an officer of the corporation; and
4. **returned to the Alberta Corporate Tax Administration promptly upon completion.**

2 Corporation Name and Address

HIGHRISE RESTAURANTS LTD.

112 Eat Hardy Drive S.W.
Calgary, Alberta   T2P 0V6

Please refer to the Information Return: Corporate Identification Guide when completing this form. If additional assistance is required telephone (403) 427-9412 or Zenith 22143.

3 Address of Principal Alberta Business Location (If different from the Address in area 2 above)	**4** Mailing Address (if different from the Address in area 2 above)
600-6 Avenue S.W.	same as #2
1504 Highrise Commercial Centre	
Calgary, Alberta T2P 0X4 Postal Code	Postal Code

5 Telephone Number   (at mailing address)   4 0 3 (Area Code)   2 6 9 1 1 1 1 (Telephone Number)

6 Corporation Federal Income Tax Account Number   unknown

7 Taxation Year End   3 1   D E C   (eg. 31-Dec.)
Day   Month

8 Location of Head Office   1   (Alberta = 1; Other Canadian location = 2; Other = 3)

9 Corporation Operating Status within Alberta   1   (Operating = 1; Non-Operating = 2)

10 Describe the nature of business from which the corporation's chief source of income is derived: Restaurant

11 List the principal product(s) manufactured or sold, or service(s) provided: Food and Beverages

12 Select the Standard Industrial Classification (SIC) Code which best describes your operation: 9 2 1 1   (Refer to guide for codes)

13 Type of Corporation (as defined in guide)   1   Canadian controlled private (excluding Alberta professional) = 1; Alberta professional = 2; Other private = 3; Public = 4; Other = 5; (if 5, specify)

14 If your corporation wishes to be included on a mailing list for receipt of Alberta corporate tax information, check (✓) the box to the right.   ✓

15 Certification of Information:

STEW COOKE   PRESIDENT
Name of Officer (please print)   Position (please print)

I am an authorized signing officer of the corporation. I certify that this Information Return: Corporate Identification has been examined by me, and is a true, correct and complete return.

Date: _____   Signature: _____

For Office Use Only

Initials: _____

Date:

3. Municipal requirements and regulations

The following are some of the more important municipal government requirements that may affect your business.

(a) The licensing of businesses

Every municipality has the right to require a business located within its boundaries to obtain a valid business licence. Coupled with that right is the right the municipalities have to control the zoning and use of land.

The municipality can determine what types of businesses will be allowed in particular areas and can impose restrictions or attach guidelines affecting the business. Examples of these restrictions include size or location of business premises, Sunday shopping or other restrictive by-laws, and food, health, and fire regulations.

Contact your local city hall, business licence department, and planning department to obtain further information.

(b) Municipal taxation

Municipalities have the right to assess and collect taxes based mainly on real estate and business tax evaluations. As well, in conjunction with the local school authority, the municipality collects additional assessments to be used for educational purposes.

You have the right to appeal these assessments if you think they have been improperly allocated. The appeal procedure will involve a hearing before the relevant taxing authority. Details can be provided by the municipal office.

(c) Building requirements

The municipality, through its building and planning department, regulates the construction and maintenance of buildings. Building and development permits must be obtained from the municipality prior to construction of a new building or an addition or renovation to an existing building.

As well, the municipality imposes ongoing safety and maintenance regulations designed to keep the buildings in a safe and functional condition.

b. INTRODUCTION TO SECURITIES LAW

As mentioned in several previous chapters, the scope of this book is designed to deal with the small non-distributing company. However, it is useful to have at least some knowledge about the Securities Act.

Basically, the act provides that no person or company shall trade in a security unless that person or company is registered with the Securities Commission; no trading can take place in that security unless a preliminary prospectus has been filed and approved by the Securities Commission.

For our purposes it is important to note that the definition of a "security" includes a share. Accordingly, you should be aware that you cannot trade your shares publicly without considering the requirements of the Securities Act.

I have mentioned several times the importance of including a restriction on the transfer of shares in your Articles of Incorporation. One reason why such a restriction should be imposed is to ensure that the sale of shares in a non-distributing company does not qualify as a trade to the public.

In addition to the above, a security problem may arise when an existing company attempts to raise money by selling shares. This is known as a "distribution." Unless your company wants to go through a long complicated and expensive filing procedure, it had better ensure that it is not breaching the terms of the Securities Act.

The act does provide certain guidelines which allow a private placement of funds in the company without the necessity of having a prospectus approved. If raising funds by a distribution of this type is being contemplated by your company, I recommend that you obtain legal advice.

Securities legislation should not, however, affect the situation where a small number of personal friends or relatives are approached to buy shares or contribute money to the company.

c. HOW CAN I BORROW MONEY FOR THE COMPANY?

One of the most fundamental and practical problems that you may be faced with is how to raise money. Although adept at carrying on your business when it comes to dealing with lending institutions, you may be at a loss about how to make the most of the assets that are at your disposal.

In this section, I will deal briefly with the various types of security that are available to you and to the company if it is necessary to borrow money.

1. Sale of shares

A company can raise money by the sale of its shares; in fact, this is how many large companies raise money from the public on the stock market through preliminary distributions or private placements. The advantage of raising money this way is that it does not involve the repayment of interest nor does it require the company to put up any additional security.

The disadvantage of equity financing, as this is called, is that issuing additional shares will bring in other shareholders to the company and could either affect the control block of the company or dilute the interests of the existing shareholders. I have also noted the securities problem that could be raised when the sale of a security is concerned.

Finally, potential investors in a company may not wish to purchase shares but would rather lend the monies to the company. The reason for this is that if the investors put their money in as share capital,

they not only put that money at risk, but because of the concept of limited liability, they will be one of the last people on the totem pole to recoup their investment if the company goes under, because they will collect only after all the secured and preferred creditors have been paid.

2. Promissory note

In most cases, when a company first begins dealing with a lending institution, it starts off with a loan or a small line of credit in the amount of $5 000 or $10 000. The line of credit is normally secured simply by one or a series of demand promissory notes that are left with the bank and processed each time the company needs monies.

The promissory note is basically a contract between the company and the lender; the company promises to repay the debt in accordance with the terms of the note. In all cases, the note will contain a provision outlining the interest repayment and will either be payable on demand (as was the situation with Mrs. Cooke) or at a specifically appointed time.

If the company does not pay back the note when demanded or at the appointed time, the company is in default and may be sued by the lender. The advantage for the lender of taking a promissory note is that, if there is a default, the lender can begin and maintain legal action on the promissory note itself. This is particularly important because a promissory note is designed to be easily "negotiated" between parties.

Negotiation is a complex legal concept, but basically it is designed to allow notes to be transferred or sold from party to party. Special rules have been developed to ensure that certain parties who acquire promissory notes, known as "holders in due course," are not affected by any potential flaws or defects in the promissory note or in the contract between the original parties.

For example, assume that Company A purchases $10 000 worth of stock from Manufacturer B and instead of paying cash, gives Manufacturer B a promissory note for $10 000. Now assume that of the goods received by Company A, $2 500 worth of the goods were damaged. However, before A told B about the damaged goods, B "negotiated" the promissory note to its creditor, C, for a discounted but fair value price of $8 000. The note is now held by C. When it comes time for Company A to repay the note, Creditor C will be entitled to the full $10 000 plus interest from Company A as long as Creditor C had no previous knowledge that some of the goods delivered by B to Company A were damaged. Company A's only recourse is to go back against Manufacturer B for the $2 500 that it has had to pay to Creditor C.

This concept of negotiability is extremely important in any commercial transaction and provides excellent security to the ultimate holder of the note. However, except as noted above, a note holder is not a secured creditor.

3. Land mortgage

If the company owns any land in its own name, it can borrow against that land to the value of its equity. Equity is normally defined as the difference between the fair market value of the land less any existing mortgages or encumbrances against the property.

For example, if a company owns a piece of land worth $100 000, which is subject to a first mortgage for $40 000, it has an equity of $60 000. Theoretically, the company could borrow up to $60 000 against the equity in the property and provide good security in the land to the lender.

In practical terms, most lenders will only lend up to approximately 75% or 80% of the land value in order to protect themselves against any possible decline in the value of land. The security document involved is known as a land mortgage. It is signed by

the company and registered against the title to the land. Once registered, that mortgage has a priority against any subsequent claims that are registered on the title.

If there is a default in payment of monies due on the mortgage, the lender has the right of foreclosure against the land. In this procedure, if the loan is not paid up within a period of time set by the court (the redemption period), the property can be advertised for sale and sold, with the proceeds used to pay off the lender.

If the property is advertised for sale and there are no offers, then the lender is entitled to apply to the court for a final order of foreclosure, which will put title of the property into the name of the lender and thereby extinguish the debt.

A land mortgage is a very common and valuable type of asset but, subject to the comments below about collateral security, it is only effective if the company itself owns the land.

4. Chattel mortgage

A chattel mortgage is similar to a land mortgage except that instead of being registered by way of a General Security Agreement against land, it is registered against particular pieces of equipment owned by the company. For example, a chattel mortgage may be registered against vehicles, manufacturing equipment, inventory, fixtures, etc.

The chattel mortgage (General Security Agreement) is registered at the Personal Property Registration Branch office in Alberta. From the date of registration, it gives a priority to the chattel mortgagee (the lender).

If there is a default, the lender has the right to have the sheriff seize the secured equipment and have it sold in an auction, with the proceeds being used to repay the debt.

The chattel mortgagee is a secured creditor and has a priority to that equipment over any other unsecured creditor who may have a claim against the company or its assets.

5. General security agreement

The general security agreement is the most popular type of security available to corporations because of the flexibility it provides to both the lender and the borrower.

In essence, the general security agreement is a form of security that, unlike the mortgage which must specify the assets used as security, covers all the assets of the borrower in a "floating" charge. This floating security usually charges everything owned by the borrower, now, or in the future, including all inventory, stock, real and personal property, and fixtures, but allows the borrower to use those assets in the ordinary course of business.

However, on default, the lender has the right to "crystallize" the general security agreement and appoint a receiver manager. The crystallization of the general security agreement means that when the lender tells the borrower that the loan is in default, all of the assets then owned by the borrower become frozen and available to the lender to repay the debt.

The lender has the right to place the business into "receivership" and either sell any of the assets to satisfy the debt or continue to run the business in an attempt to pay back the money that is owing.

The general security agreement is registered at the Personal Property Securities Registry through a private registry office. If the agreement covers land, it is also registered at the Land Titles Office.

Because this form of security is quite complicated, legal assistance should be obtained if only to ensure that the clauses in the general security agreement are ones you can live with.

6. Assignment of book debts

Many businesses rely on their accounts receivable to generate their cash flow. These receivables can be a valuable form of security, and lenders will lend on the strength of the amount of the receivables that you have.

The normal form of security that is taken is called an assignment of book debts and is registered at the Personal Property Registry. The effect of the assignment of book debts is that once registered, the lender has priority to those accounts receivable against all other creditors.

In a default, the lender need only give notice to the various accounts who owe money to the company. They are then obliged to pay the monies directly to the lender and not to the borrower.

7. Section 178 security

Under the Federal Bank Act, banks are authorized to lend monies to those individuals or companies involved in primary industries. In other words, loans can be made to the fishing, farming, manufacturing, and lumber industries with the security being simply the harvest or final manufactured goods to be produced from the raw materials.

The security is registered at the Bank of Canada and is known as a section 178 security. It is very much like the General Security Agreement in that it allows the borrower to use and work with inventory without any interference whatsoever. But in a default, the lender has a right to all of the finished goods to satisfy the debt.

8. Personal guarantee

Many lending institutions recognize the fact that a company may simply be a device that an individual is using to obtain the benefits of limited liability. Often times, all the assets that are in the company are in as shareholders' loan and the company itself, especially in its initial stages, does not have the asset value to support a loan.

In these situations, the lending institution will normally require that the individuals behind the company personally guarantee the repayment of the loan in order to provide them with a second source of security.

In Alberta, these personal guarantees are very common and required almost as of right by the lending institutions.

Under Alberta law, it is very important that a person signing a personal guarantee go to a notary public (who is usually a lawyer) and sign an acknowledgment on the back of the guarantee. This is required by law to make the individual aware that he or she is assuming personal liability for the debts of the company if the company cannot pay. If that acknowledgment is not attached to the guarantee, the guarantee is invalid.

9. Collateral security

As well as requiring personal guarantees, lenders also look at other security that the individuals behind companies may have to offer. Often the lenders will require what is known as collateral security from the individuals even though the loan is being made to the company.

Collateral security is basically security which is "collateral" or secondary to the prime security that the lender has insisted on. For example, a lender who makes a loan of $50 000 to a company in a promissory note may take as additional security a collateral mortgage on the residence of the prime shareholder.

In effect, therefore, the lender not only has the promissory note from the company as security to satisfy the debt, but also the personal residence of the individual shareholder. The mortgage against the individual's residence is known as the collateral security.

Collateral security may take many, many forms and, of course, depends on the asset position of the company and its shareholders. The example noted above merely illustrates how it works. A common rule of thumb is that the larger the loan, or the

greater the risk, the more security the lender requires.

10. Franchises Act

Franchising is a popular way of doing business today. The intent of this section is to introduce you to the subject, as most franchises are operated as corporations rather than as sole proprietorships or partnerships. Although there is a lot to learn about franchises, it remains outside the scope of this book to discuss them in great detail. However, if you want more indepth information on the topic, see another title in the Self-Counsel Series, *Franchising in Canada*.

A franchise consists of a franchisor, that has developed or owns assets which comprise a business system, along with one or more franchisees, who "rent" the right to use that system to run a business in a particular location. The assets usually include recognizable names, logos, trade marks, patents, trade secrets (such as recipes for particular foods), accounting systems, and specialized products or services.

As a franchisee, you will typically pay the franchisor an up-front fee for the right to do business under its licence. You will then have to set up your business as required by the franchisor, usually in a location owned or leased by the franchisor and then leased or sub-leased to you. Usually, you must purchase all products and services for the franchise from the franchisor, which receives, in addition to payment for the products or services that you buy from it, an ongoing royalty payment out of your gross profits.

Although every franchise is different, they do have one thing in common — a lot of paper for you to review and sign! Sound advice, from both a lawyer and an accountant familiar with the franchise business operation, is advisable and well worth the cost.

Alberta is unique in that legislation of franchises has been in force for several years. The laws were changed dramatically in 1995 to make Alberta a more competitive jurisdiction for prospective franchise operations. However, there are still plenty of teeth in the legislation to protect your interests when you purchase a franchise.

The most important aspect of the legislation is the "disclosure document," which the franchisor must provide. This document details the franchise operation and includes financial information about the franchisor. Any material misstatements or omissions in this document give you the right to cancel your agreement with the franchisor and get your money back, even after you have set up your business. Naturally, you should spend time reviewing the disclosure document and asking a lot of questions about any matters you don't understand.

Most franchisors prefer that franchises, or assets used to run a franchise (such as kitchen equipment), are owned through a corporation. Franchisors and banks encourage this arrangement, as it gives them two legal entities — you and your corporation — to pursue if default occurs. Given, however, that you may not be able to avoid this, you should structure your company in such a way as to take full advantage of all legal and tax benefits available to you.

For example, if your spouse will be working with you in the business, make sure that he or she owns some shares. This will allow you to split profits with your spouse by dividing income between you, and therefore keeping your tax rate low. Also, if you are transferring vehicles into the company, or any other assets that may be worth more now than what you originally paid for them, or how they appear in your books, make sure you do it by way of a section 85 rollover agreement.

Finally, I recommend that you set up a new company with the sole function of owning and operating the franchise. This way, if it doesn't work out, other assets that you own personally or in another company aren't endangered. If you *do* have another company, make sure that you set up your "franchise" company in such a way that you don't jeopardize the small business tax rate for both companies by making the two companies "associated" for tax purposes. This can usually be accomplished by ensuring that your shareholdings in both companies are less than 50%.

10

CONCLUSION

At the beginning of this book I congratulated you for making the decision to go into business. After having read through this book, you may appreciate now why congratulations were extended to you. Translating a basic idea that you think can generate some revenue into an actual business supported in most cases by a limited company can be a trying, difficult experience. Many times you will feel like a salmon swimming upstream.

However, it is people like you who keep our economy buoyant and, to a great extent, preserve the way of life that we have and that we often take for granted. The rewards may certainly be substantial but there is no easy route to achieving them. Invariably, the journey to success includes a tremendous amount of personal sacrifice, expense, and basic hard work.

It is hoped that this book has served to smooth that journey for you by providing a wide range of information about how to deal with the problems that you may encounter along your way. I stress that this book should not be looked on as a substitute for having your own corporate solicitor, accountant, or any other source of advice that you may have at your disposal.

In conclusion, I have listed below various sources of information that you may wish to call upon from time to time in operating your business. And may I say to you once again — Congratulations!

(a) Bank manager: Your bank manager has available a tremendous amount of information regarding not only general financing, but also specific information which may affect your business.

(b) Business Development Bank of Canada and Alberta Opportunity Company: These are government funded organizations that will lend monies to businesses in situations where other lending institutions will not; they also provide several services to assist business people in operating their companies and often provide seminars on various aspects of business which may be of interest to you.

(c) Universities and secondary schools: Often the continuing education divisions of universities and secondary schools will run one- or two-day seminars on particular aspects of business; you should contact the administration offices of the institutions in your area to find out what they have to offer.

(d) Check your local newspapers for seminars that are run by private individuals and organizations; these seminars are geared for business people and cover topics ranging from tax savings to business planning and investment opportunities.

(e) Government offices: Most government offices maintain a public relations or public information department and have literature available for public distribution about particular aspects of business.

(f) Business associations or groups: Many business people in a common business enterprise join together in associations to provide a stronger voice in government and to provide self-government or assistance to members; they often have at their fingertips tremendous amounts of information.

(g) Professional sources: Don't discount the information, experience, and knowledge of many accountants and lawyers currently practising in Alberta; many have practical business experience as well as academic knowledge and should be consulted from time to time. In fact, you'll often be pleasantly surprised with the co-operation and information you'll get with little or no cost to you.

(h) The Internet: You can now "surf the net" and discover all sorts of useful information on every aspect of your business. If you can tap into someone else's expertise to make your road a little smoother, go for it!

APPENDIX 1
CHECKLIST OF STEPS TO BE FOLLOWED

_____ Select a name for your corporation. If possible, check the microfiche maintained by the Corporate Registry to determine whether your proposed name, or a name similar to it, has already been incorporated.

_____ Reserve your name with the Private Sector Service Centre and obtain NUANS report from name search firm.

_____ Purchase package of forms or software (see order form at front of book)

_____ Prepare Articles of Incorporation, Notice of Registered Office, and Notice of Appointment of Directors.

_____ Forward the following documents to the Corporate Registry in Edmonton:

    (a) NUANS report

    (b) Articles of Incorporation and all schedules

    (c) Notice of Registered Office

    (d) $300 filing fee*

    (e) Request for Services form — available from the Corporate Registry.

_____ Acquire Corporate Seal and Minute Book with tabs or dividers for specific filings.

_____ Insert approved corporate documents in the Minute Book when they are returned from the Corporate Registry.

_____ Prepare the following minutes:

    (a) Incorporators' minutes

    (b) Meeting of first shareholders

    (c) Meeting of first directors

_____ Prepare share subscriptions for all shares (common or preferred) that are to be issued to initial investors.

_____ Issue share certificates and update share register, share transfer register (if necessary), and individual shareholder registers.

_____ File any Amended Notices with the Corporate Registry if necessary.

_____ Obtain banking documents from the bank where your corporate account is to be maintained and complete all banking resolutions.

_____ Prepare any agreements or promissory notes and issue any shares necessary for the sale or transfer of personal assets to your corporation. If the transfer involves any rollover documentation, prepare and file all Revenue Canada filings.

_____ Apply for and obtain all necessary business licences, provincial approvals, Workers' Compensation number, and GST number as may be applicable.

_____ Choose your corporate year end. Set up a diary system to note filing dates for filing the Annual Return, provincial and federal tax filings, licence renewals, etc.

_____ Find a good accountant/bookkeeper to help set up financial records and other accounting matters relating to the business carried on by your corporation.

_____ Commence carrying on business, and make it a huge success!

---

*Fees are subject to change without notice. Always check with the Corporate Registry first before submitting any fees.

APPENDIX 2
INCORPORATION FEE SCHEDULE

1.	Certificate of Incorporation	$300
2.	Certificate of Amalgamation	300
3.	Certificate of Registration of an Extra-provincial Corporation	300
4.	Change of name for an extra-provincial corporation	75
5.	Certificate of Amendment of Registration of an Extra-provincial Corporation	75
6.	Certificate of Registration of an Amalgamated Corporation (Extra-provincial)	300
7.	Certificate of Restated Articles of Incorporation	75
8.	Certificate of Continuance under section 181	300
9.	Certificate of Amendment (articles of reorganization)	75
10.	Certificate of Revival	300
11.	Certificate of Revocation of Intent to Dissolve	50
12.	Certificate of English/French Name Equivalency or Pseudonym	50
13.	Certificate of Continuance under section 261	300
14.	Certificate of Dissolution	50
15.	Revocation of Intent to Dissolve	50
16.	Change of Name	75
17.	To accompany annual return sent to Registrar	20
18.	Any certificate or certification for which a fee is not provided	25
*19.	Search — for each corporation (microfiche only)	10
*20.	Certification:	
	Certificate	25
	Each page certified	1
*21.	Uncertified copy of any document or part of a document, per page	1
22.	Appointment of a receiver	20
*23.	Comfiche	
24.	Corrected certificate	75
25.	Photocopy of the Registrar's register of mortgages, per page	1
26.	Monthly listing of receiver and receiver-manager appointments filed with the Registrar, per month	50
27.	Facsimile transfer, for each corporation	5

For expedited service on any of these items, double the fee listed and indicate your wish for expedited service in your covering letter.

*GST applies to these services and to the expedited portion of any service.

OTHER TITLES IN THE SELF-COUNSEL BUSINESS SERIES

BASIC ACCOUNTING FOR THE SMALL BUSINESS

Simple, foolproof techniques for keeping your books straight and staying out of trouble

Clive Cornish, C.G.A.

$7.95

Having bookkeeping problems? Do you feel you should know more about bookkeeping, but simply don't have time for a course? Do you wish that the paperwork in your business could be improved, but you don't know where or how to start?

This book is a down-to-earth manual on how to save your accountant's time and your time and money. Written in clear, everyday English, not in accounting jargon, this guide will help you and your office staff keep better records.

Inside you will find illustrations of sample forms and instructions on how to prepare all the records you will need to keep, including:

- Daily cash sheet
- Cash summary
- Statement ledger
- Payables journal
- Synoptic journal
- Payroll book
- Income statement
- Trial balance
- Columnar work sheet

PREPARING A SUCCESSFUL BUSINESS PLAN

A practical guide for small business

Rodger Touchie, B.Comm., M.B.A.

$14.95

At some time, every business needs a formal business plan. Whether considering a new business venture or rethinking an existing one, an effective plan is essential to success. From start to finish, this working guide outlines how to prepare a plan that will win potential investors and help achieve business goals.

Using worksheets and a sample plan, readers learn how to create an effective plan, establish planning and maintenance methods, and update their strategy in response to actual business conditions.

Contents include:

- The basic elements of business planning
- The company and its product
- The marketing plan
- The financial plan
- The team
- Concluding remarks and appendixes
- The executive summary
- Presenting an impressive document
- Common misconceptions in business planning
- Your business plan as a tangible asset

STANDARD LEGAL FORMS AND AGREEMENTS

Steve Sanderson, editor

$14.95

This book provides a wide selection of indispensable legal forms and common business agreements ready to be copied and filled in with the particulars of the arrangement. It features a lay-flat binding and all samples are provided full-size in this large format volume so that no fussing with enlargements is necessary and copying is both easy and perfect quality.

Contents include:

- New businesses — agreement of purchase — partnership agreement
- Services — engagement of services
- Employment — employment agreement — employee dismissal letter
- Buying — invitation to quote — cancellation of purchase order
- Selling — bill of sale — limited warranty
- Collections — request for payment — bad cheque letter
- Credit/Debit — personal credit application — guarantee
- Leases — commercial lease — agreement to cancel lease
- Assignments — assignment with warranties — assignment of contract

ORDER FORM

All prices are subject to change without notice. Books are available in book, department, and stationery stores. If you cannot buy the book through a store, please use this order form. (Please print)

Name _____

Address _____

_____

Charge to: ❑ Visa   ❑ MasterCard

Account Number _____

Validation Date _____

Expiry Date _____

Signature _____

YES, please send me:

_____ **Basic Accounting for the Small Business** $8.95

_____ **Preparing a Successful Business Plan** $14.95

_____ **Standard Legal Forms and Agreements** $14.95

Please add $3.00 for postage and handling. Canadian residents, please add 7% GST to your order.

❑ **Check here for a free catalogue.**

Please send your order to:

Self-Counsel Press
1481 Charlotte Road
North Vancouver, B. C.
V7J 1H1

Visit our Internet Web Site at:
http://www.self-counsel.com/